TONY RICKSON

The joy
of football
celebrations

First published by Pitch Publishing, 2020

Pitch Publishing
A2 Yeoman Gate
Yeoman Way
Worthing
Sussex
BN13 3QZ
www.pitchpublishing.co.uk
info@pitchpublishing.co.uk

A CIP catalogue record is available for this book
from the British Library.

ISBN 978 1 78531 730 9

Typesetting and origination by Pitch Publishing
Printed and bound in India by Replika Press Pvt. Ltd.

Contents

Acknowledgements

THANK YOU to Frances Rickson, Jessica Rickson, Will Rickson and Geoff Rickson for all their support, advice, comments, knowledge and suggestions.

Thank you also to everybody and anybody who has ever shared information about football celebrations. This includes broadcasters, writers for local and national newspapers, websites and books, football supporters and clubs, and those posting online with YouTube, Twitter, Instagram etc.

Thank you also to Katie Field, Graham Hales, Duncan Olner and Dean Rockett, and all the team at Pitch Publishing, for making this book happen.

1

Great goal, great celebration

HERE WE are at the world's most iconic football stadium, and it's a beautiful sunny summer Saturday afternoon. No, not that one, though we'll come to it in a minute.

This was Thirty Years of Hurt later – 15 June 1996. The occasion was the European Championships and England were playing at Wembley against their oldest footballing rivals, Scotland. The build-up to the goal was exquisite, the execution was jaw-droppingly stunning, and the celebration was ... well, the best there's ever been. Before, obviously, but since too, although a lot more effort and work has gone into the apparently simple goal celebration ever since.

The lead was a narrow 1-0 to England with 11 minutes to go when goalkeeper David Seaman launched a long ball forward, route-one style. A couple of quick passes on, and Paul Gascoigne cut in from what we used to call the inside-left position. With his left foot he lifted the ball cleverly over Scotland defender Colin Hendry and as it fell he volleyed it with his right to send it sizzling inside the near post past his Glasgow Rangers team-mate, keeper Andy Goram. What a manoeuvre. What a strike. What a match-clinching goal.

Gascoigne had his wits about him when he created and scored that perfect goal, and he had his wits about him to remember how he'd planned to celebrate if such a glorious moment arose. He raced beyond the far post to lie on his back with his arms outstretched. Team-mates in on the joke ran to squeeze handily-placed water bottles into Gazza's wide open mouth. A few seconds, no more, and the cameo was over and the England players were returning triumphantly to their own half.

The inspiration for the celebration was an incident a couple of weeks previously on a pre-tournament trip to Hong Kong. The players had let their hair down on a night out and Gascoigne, to no one's surprise, was in the thick of it. He found a dentist's chair in a nightclub – as you do – and laid back in it while drinks were poured into his mouth. Footballers everywhere have been known to let their hair down on the odd occasion – the problem here was the image was captured on camera and the next anyone knew it was on the front page of a national newspaper. How embarrassing. Newspaper columnists have never had a drink on a night off, of course, but were quickly into print to condemn England's thirsty footballers.

Did it spoil their performance in the upcoming Euros? Well hardly, England unluckily went out in the semi-finals in what equalled their most successful tournament since 1966. And that Gascoigne celebration was a suitably stinging but tongue-in-cheek response to the criticism.

His Wembley celebration told a story and was smart, quick and funny. And it wasn't the first time a passionate Gascoigne had moved a multi-million TV audience. He'd done it in 1990, too, when he wept after getting booked in the World Cup semi-final against West Germany, meaning he would have missed the final if England had qualified. (They didn't!)

Gazza's emotional and unforgettable moments were of extra significance as football in England had endured a miserable previous decade. Hundreds of innocent lives had been lost at Hillsborough, Heysel and Bradford. Prime Minister Margaret Thatcher hated the game, and football, beset by hooliganism, was at its lowest ebb. It needed to rediscover what we'd always loved about it – the passion, the excitement, the fun, the emotion.

Several things combined to create the renaissance. There was the heart-warming Italia 90 World Cup, with Gazza's tears touching us all. There was the re-admittance of English clubs into European competitions, the start of the Premier League, and the publication of seminal football book *Fever Pitch*. (Who could forget the young lad reluctantly dragged along to his first match at Arsenal, and as he goes into the stadium becoming so overwhelmed by the noise, the anticipation, the smell, the excitement, the green grass, that he asks his dad: 'Who are we playing next week?')

Celebrations helped as well. After Arsenal had stunningly beaten Liverpool 2-0 at Anfield to clinch the 1989 Division One championship on goals scored, home fans stayed behind to acknowledge their achievement and applaud them as they celebrated. Where so recently there had been hooliganism and bitter confrontation, suddenly it was being replaced by respect and sportsmanship.

So the drama and the passion were gradually returning to the beautiful game. Once upon a time, a polite handshake was the absolute furthest a team-mate would go in the form of congratulations after a goal had been scored. The scorer himself would march back to the halfway line, pleased with himself inwardly, but programmed not to show pleasure on the outside. Cool, calm, don't show your emotions; stiff upper lip and all that.

So often since those far-off days, it's the celebrations we remember more than the goal itself. Gascoigne's wasn't the first, but suddenly every time someone scored we began to look for what they were going to do. Thought was going into it and there were dozens of ways to enhance the moment. The knee-slide. The aeroplane. The bundle. Rocking a baby. Or sucking a thumb. Pointing – at the club badge, at a team-mate, at their own name on the back of their shirt, at a partner in the stand, or to the sky to remember a departed loved one. Kissing a camera. Some form of acrobatics. Forming a love-heart with the hands. Dancing around a corner flag. An annoying shushing gesture. An equally annoying cocky look. Shirt over the face. Or shirt off altogether.

One thing we'd never thought of, though, was revealed by Arsenal and England defender Martin Keown, in his post-retirement work in the media. He reported in the *Daily Mail* that Arsenal manager Arsene Wenger had questioned why he was only covering 10 kilometres in a match. Keown wrote: 'So I started celebrating the goals. I'd sprint to the other end of the pitch to be with my team-mates and suddenly I was hitting 11km, 11.5km. Job done.'

Take a look, yet another look, at the goals when England won the 1966 World Cup at Wembley on that previous summery sunny Saturday afternoon. The scorer would manage an involuntary little leap, and raise one, or both, arms. Those nearest would offer congratulations but defenders back in the day hardly ever ventured over the halfway line for any reason, and certainly not to acknowledge a goal. Now one's hardly ever scored without the whole team bundling into a celebration, the scorer often buried deep at the bottom of the heap. Rarely the goalkeeper, though; it usually looks naff if they break ranks to race up and join in. However, this book has uncovered the occasional exception to that rule. And what do kids kicking about in the park and the junior leagues do? They copy everything and do it with feeling. A game doesn't go by without a knee slide. Or that cupping-ears gesture. Professionals as role models? They surely are.

What our youngsters must be discouraged from doing are the celebrations that are horribly wrong. The odd Nazi salute has crept in over the years, as has the quenelle, a nasty anti-Semitic gesture. As well as players forming their hands to depict handcuffs in solidarity with, perhaps, a friend who had been sent to prison. Referees are instructed to issue bookings for shirt removal, going into the crowd, revealing a t-shirt with a political or unsuitable message and taunting opposition fans in an unacceptable way.

There was no way Marco Tardelli was going to produce an inappropriate goal celebration when he scored for Italy against West Germany on their way to victory in the 1982 World Cup Final. Caught up in the moment, he just raced away, fists clenched, tear-stained face taut with a manic expression, probably becoming the first man in history to heartlessly brush aside excited team-mates as if they'd had nothing to do with it. Many reckoned it was the most goosebump-worthy goal celebration ever. His was a great example of the involuntary celebration. Tardelli never planned it that way, the moment just overwhelmed him.

Goalscorers began to run faster and faster in jubilation, but the arrival of the 1990s saw a change, with the addition of the pre-planned celebration. As well as Gascoigne, there was Jurgen Klinsmann's self-mocking dive after scoring on his Spurs debut, Roger Milla doing sexy dancing round the corner flag, and Brazil's Bebeto introducing that oh-so-sweet but still slightly nauseating baby-rocking routine in 1994. The new baby in question, by the way, is now … guess what: a professional footballer.

By coincidence, it was Brazil who featured in what became one of the most famous non-celebrations in another World Cup, in 2014. Germany gave them a 7-1 semi-final thrashing and decided to stop celebrating their goals out of respect for what Brazil had achieved in football. Players, of course, have been known to refrain from celebrating if they've put one over their former club – Frank Lampard against Chelsea while enjoying a short period at Manchester City in 2014/15 is one of hundreds of examples. So there was only one way for Lampard to turn after scoring. On his heels and back to the halfway line.

Which doesn't solve the problem all players face about which way to, well, face, once they've scored. Should they run towards their colleagues, who clearly must have played some part in creating the goal? Or should they go to the fans, who have paid a lot of money to be there to enjoy such a moment? Didier Drogba, for instance, would always head towards the supporters to salute them, and didn't Chelsea fans love him all the more for that? On the other hand, Thierry Henry usually turned inwards to point at the team-mate who had set him up. Steven Gerrard, meanwhile, had a knack of knowing where the nearest camera was to slide towards and smother with a passionate little kiss.

Celebrations? We love them. Wolves manager Nuno Espirito Santo, talking about delays caused by VAR decision-making which marred the 2019/20 Premier League season (before coronavirus ruined it some more!) called them the most important moments in football. This book is packed with hundreds of them: some you'll remember vividly, others will ring a bell in the back of the mind. If it was good, it'll be here somewhere. To the players, keep them coming and keep them innovative. Who knows if in the next game we watch, someone will come up with something we've simply never seen before …

2

Funny moments:
You're having a laugh

HE HAD more opportunities than almost anyone to perfect a trademark celebration. Trouble is, Wayne Rooney was usually so pleased at scoring that he neglected to do anything special. OK, the man who ended up captain of both England and Manchester United has done somersaults, knee-slides, jumping, pointing, kissing and waving, but mostly just sprinting away with both arms outstretched after scoring another goal in a long and successful career.

It all started when he announced himself in October 2002 as a 16-year-old for Everton with a superb goal against Arsenal. With the score at 1-1 he picked up the ball more than 30 yards out and advanced before hitting a tremendous right-footer inside the near post. The goal ended Arsenal's 30-match unbeaten run and also made Rooney the youngest goalscorer in Premier League history. But that day he was so busy enjoying the moment he was mobbed by his ecstatic Everton team-mates before he could do anything much in terms of celebration.

England's all-time record goalscorer, Rooney subsequently got into trouble for one of his more exuberant celebration moments. It was 2 April 2011, the day he got his 100th goal in the Premier League, as Manchester United came from two down to win 4-2 away to West Ham. During his celebrations, he swore into a pitchside camera and was subsequently suspended for using offensive language.

It was all of 13 years after that stunning winner for Everton against Arsenal that Rooney unveiled a pre-planned goal celebration. One that we like to call a 'topical'. It followed a clip of a home video which showed Rooney being floored by a punch while mucking about doing boxing in his kitchen at home with his ex-Manchester United colleague Phil Bardsley and probably some other mates, too. He was such a household name that the sight of him laid out on the floor ended up on the front page of a national newspaper. A keen boxing fan who was involved in the sport as a youngster, Rooney maintained it was just a bit of fun and he wasn't hurt in the incident. There was a lot of faux tut-tutting about setting a poor example, and all that. As if we ought not to be able to mess around in the privacy of our own homes.

But Rooney showed what he thought of the criticism when he scored the following week, on 15 March 2015, for Manchester United against Spurs at

Old Trafford. Spurs gave the ball away and Rooney bore down on goal before slotting calmly beyond keeper Hugo Lloris. To celebrate, he took up a boxer's stance, did a bit of shadow boxing with three or four punches, and then crashed backwards on to the turf, pretending to be knocked out. Great fun and a great image. Rooney 1 Critics 0.

They're different characters, but there were great similarities between Rooney's set piece and the one by Paul Gascoigne at Wembley in 1996. Both were in response to an 'exclusive' in a national newspaper purporting to show them in a bad light, and both were clever, topical, pointed and, above all, funny. And both ended with them flat on their backs!

Later in the book, we'll come to the more serious celebrations that have ended in injury or sparked controversy, but this is the fun chapter, the moments that have made us laugh out loud. So step forward Jimmy Bullard, and a glance at the fans behind him celebrating after scoring a penalty for Hull City at Manchester City tells you everything. They're roaring their heads off. And it's undeniably one of the funniest goal celebrations ever.

The story began the previous season on Boxing Day 2008 when Hull were thrashed 5-1 on the same ground. Instead of marching his players off to the dressing room for a half-time dressing down, when they were already four goals behind, manager Phil Brown sat them down on the Eastlands pitch and, in full view of everybody, gave them all a finger-wagging ear-bashing. It was humiliating and embarrassing for the players, and Brown was heavily criticised at the time, but it was obviously a lesson that wasn't forgotten.

Because when Bullard scored the next season – the match on 28 November 2009 ended 1-1 – he replicated the scene. His colleagues sat down like little boys on the pitch and Bullard, one of football's most renowned jokers, did his very best Phil Brown impression and wagged his finger at them one by one. The big question was: how would the boss take it? To much relief all round among the players, Brown thought the mickey-take was hilarious. 'It was a fantastic celebration,' he generously told the BBC. 'Great comedy is about timing. I couldn't deliver my post-match speech as I was laughing so much. The whole thing was timed to perfection. You couldn't have had a celebration like that unless it was at Eastlands and in the goal in front of the Hull fans. I had no idea it was going to happen. I was trying to arrange a five-man midfield at the time so I didn't see it.'

Bullard recalled the moment in his book, *Bend It Like Bullard*. 'We had agreed that whoever scored an equaliser or winning goal had to be the one who did the pointing. I'd completely lost the plot, as I do whenever I score, until one of the boys reminded me about the special celebration. Within a couple of seconds, all my team-mates were sat around me in a circle while I stood in the middle, gesturing, pointing and finger-wagging. It was a pretty convincing impression of the gaffer even if I do say so myself. To add to the authenticity of this performance, it was in exactly the same spot at the same end as Brown's barmy moment the season before. I love scoring goals and I love celebrating them. I still wanted to do my own little piece where I run to all four corners of the ground acknowledging the crowd. Unfortunately, there wasn't much time for that as, for some weird reason, the referee who had so kindly given us the penalty was now insisting that we should carry on with the last eight minutes of the game. As City kicked off again my only thought was "I hope this stays 1-1 after that celebration!"'

Manchester City manager Mark Hughes wasn't amused – he was adamant it was never a penalty in the first place.

We're not changing the subject here, but what should be the song of choice to celebrate a memorable moment in football? 'We Are The Champions' by Queen? Or perhaps 'Congratulations' by Cliff Richard? See, 'Sloop John B' just doesn't spring to mind. But that was Phil Brown's selection when the Hull City team he managed – the one we've just been talking about – kept their place in the Premier League at the end of the 2008/09 season. Despite losing 1-0 to a second-string Manchester United side, Hull escaped relegation by finishing a point above Newcastle, who were simultaneously losing to Aston Villa. Brown reckoned staying up was the greatest achievement in his managerial career and celebrated on the pitch after the game by doing his very best Beach Boys impression over the PA to a bemused crowd. The verdict on the quality of his singing? Well, don't give up the day job just yet, Phil.

It wasn't what he did, but how many, when Eddie Nketiah scored his first ever goal for Arsenal in an away match at Burnley in May 2019. He managed to perform an incredible six – count them – different celebrations before his team-mates caught up with him to congratulate him on the goal that clinched a 3-1 win. Eddie put one hand to his ear, then a finger to his lips, hit his chest, stretched his arms out, waved to the crowd to gee them up and managed to squeeze in a point upwards at the sky. Top celebrating by the youngster.

Nketiah went from six celebrations to just the one when he scored a goal in a style that reminded Arsenal fans of the legendary Thierry Henry in a 3-2 home win over Everton on 23 February 2020. Referencing Carly Rae Jepsen's 'Call Me Maybe', he pretended to get out a phone and call his mates to tell them he'd just scored.

It was obviously a bit of a trend amongst young home-grown players to celebrate with a message to their friends as that's just what Chelsea's Mason Mount did a few weeks later after scoring the first goal in a 4-0 home win over Everton. He performed a neat little palms-down, foot-tapping dance for the camera and later tweeted friends to point out he'd done the Frankenstein in their honour. So that's what it was, because to me it looked a bit like the Charleston.

There should be a rule that the only time Dad Dancing is allowed is after your team has just reached the later stages of a World Cup. That would be why Kyle Walker, John Stones and Jesse Lingard got away with it after England won through to the semi-final of the 2018 World Cup and the players celebrated a 2-0 win over Sweden with a little jig for the benefit of the many fans who had followed them to Russia. The dance was a tribute act to a memorable England team from the 1990 World Cup. Their second-round victory thanks to a late goal against Belgium was celebrated by Chris Waddle and Terry Butcher with a spot of disco dancing for the fans afterwards. There's a beautiful picture of the happy twosome giving it their all, but incongruous, too, as Waddle has already swapped his white England shirt to a red Belgian one.

Talking of Waddle and pictures, there's also a lovely one that can be found somewhere in the depths of the internet of him being confronted by a referee after scoring for Spurs against Norwich in February 1989. The referee is apparently telling Waddle to cut out his celebration – lucky that one didn't catch on or we wouldn't have a book at all!

Troy Deeney got his first professional goal – many more followed – for Walsall away to Millwall on 15 September 2007 in the 86th minute to give his team a 2-1 win. He'd been on the field just two minutes and he was only 19, but he found out a bit about himself – and about celebrations. Understandably, he was pretty animated, which, of course, infuriated Millwall fans already upset at seeing their team suffer a home defeat to a late goal. Much later in his career he told Matt Dickinson in an interview for *The Times*: 'You can imagine the abuse, it's through the roof. You ugly this, you ugly that. And I had to laugh. I did have a massive head and a skinny body then, so it was like "Yup, fair enough!"'

West Ham's Michail Antonio had shown his taste for unique celebrations after scoring in a 3-1 win over Fulham at the London Stadium in February 2019. He reproduced a scene from the film *Ali G Indahouse* when Sacha Baron Cohen's character dances with a couple of mates while dodging laser beams. Antonio admitted afterwards in a Sky Sports interview that he'd messed up the routine so he was invited to attempt to go through it again with the help of pundits Gary Neville and Jamie Carragher. Which only went to prove why they're football experts rather than backing dancers on *Strictly Come Dancing*.

Just a couple of months later, Antonio performed a peculiar celebration which he claimed showed his personality, after inflicting the first defeat on Spurs at their magnificent new £1 billion stadium. Antonio got a great goal, taking down Marko Arnautovic's cross and smashing it past Hugo Lloris to secure a 1-0 win for the Hammers. (That's two goals scored past unlucky Lloris in the same chapter!) Those of a sensitive nature might need to look away now, as Antonio performed a weird and wonderful thrusting celebration move, using arms, knees and lower body in what many thought was a hugely suggestive manner. Antonio himself said afterwards the dance was inspired by internet sensation Danrue, so that's all right.

Abroad now, Sweden to be precise, and Medi Dresevic ruined what would have been his perfect day after completing his first career hat-trick when he scored three for Norrby IF against Tvaaker in August 2016. Amusingly, he celebrated by running to the side, vaulting the fence and sitting down in the stand to join fans in clapping his goal. Poor old Medi had already been booked, though, and when he returned to the pitch he got a second yellow and was sent off. Even without him, his team went on to win 6-1 that day.

Coach Mani Gamera didn't hold back when his team Miembeni beat his former club Jang'ombe 1-0 in Zanzibar in February 2020. And his celebration in front of the stands was so enthusiastic and provocative it went viral on social media. He thumped his chest, punched the air, taunted opposition fans, did some rather indelicate thrusting moves and ended up being lifted high in the air by his team. But what earned him a fine and a six-month suspension was probably the moment in the middle of his outrageous celebration when he took his trousers down and had to be stopped by a steward from going any further.

Down in Guatemala, Luis Acuna scored a penalty for Deportivo Carcha, the only goal of the game against Deportivo Jocotan, and had the bright idea of climbing a ladder to change the scoreboard to 1-0. Good on you, Luis, the booking he got for his ingenuity was totally worth it. It's pretty much all electronic scoreboards these days and you can't fiddle with them from up a ladder.

Some celebrations are imitations of others, but it must be true to say Kevin Londono's goal celebration in a Colombian league match in May 2017 has never been repeated elsewhere. When he scored for Jaguares away to Sante Fe, Kevin lay down on a sponsor's mat behind the goal and rolled himself up in it. Not once, but five or six rolls to get well and truly tucked up. Team-mates had to help the grinning Londono out of his self-inflicted mat cocoon and he probably thought the booking he got for it was well worth it. That's a wrap, Kev.

To be fair, there was nothing very special about Mike Trebilcock's celebrations of the two goals in five minutes he scored in Everton's 3-2 win over Sheffield Wednesday in the 1966 FA Cup Final. I was behind the goal at Wembley where they went in, and Trebilcock did a nice little running air-punch jump. Two of them, which was pretty standard for the 1960s. And he was caught in the dressing room afterwards downing a pint of milk, and even though that was before Humphrey's time, it was probably just what's known as a photo opportunity. Other sorts of pints probably followed later that evening.

What was far more memorable about that Cup Final was the pitch invasion by a celebrating Everton fan who looked old enough to know better. In a scene reminiscent of one of those ancient black-and-white films he managed to take off his jacket while running at what for him was full pelt. The chasing policeman grabbed the jacket just as all the man's weight had gone out of it, and he fell flat on the ground still clutching it. A comedy classic.

And finally in this chapter of amusing moments, *Match of the Day*'s goal of the 1992/93 season was capped by one of football's most iconic celebrations. It was scored by Dalian Atkinson for Aston Villa in a 3-2 win away to Wimbledon, who were then playing at Selhurst Park. He got the ball deep in his own half, evaded three despairing tackles and, hardly pausing from running at full tilt, he chipped the ball over advancing keeper Hans Segers from 20 yards out with a sublime finish. A look of delight spread over his face as he windmilled his arm and pointed to the fans. Dean Saunders was the first to congratulate him by jumping on Atkinson's back and then out of the blue they were joined by a long-haired pitch-invading Villa fan. He was so overcome with excitement at what was truly a spectacular goal that he instinctively raced on to the field to join the celebration. But he wasn't so overcome that he forgot to bring his umbrella with him. And in a beautiful though pretty surreal moment, he held the umbrella over Saunders and Atkinson to shelter them from the rain. Two happy footballers, a fan, and a brolly keeping all three of them dry. What a beautiful picture it made.

Very sadly, Atkinson died in 2016, and he's not the only one featured in this book who has since passed away. But there's always the memory of some wonderful achievements living on. In Atkinson's case in the minds of people who were there in south London the day he got his wonder goal, by watching a video of it, or looking up online the lovely photo of the umbrella celebration.

3

Being prepared: It's down your shorts

EVERYONE LOVES a pre-planned celebration – it shows some thought has been put into our post-goal enjoyment. But bringing props out just in case you score is altogether more contentious.

Pierre-Emerick Aubameyang has form for this and he knew the moment had come when he got a goal for Arsenal against Rennes in the Europa League quarter-final on 14 March 2019. Conveniently hidden behind an advertisement hoarding was a scary-looking Black Panther mask. He put it on and ran off, to the delight of his team-mates. And he also performed a crossed-armed Wakanda Forever salute – more about that in a minute. The Black Panthers is the nickname of the Gabon national team and Aubameyang explained afterwards that he needed a mask that represented him. He'd worn masks previously in his career – he was Spiderman at

Saint-Etienne and Batman when he was playing for Dortmund. Apart from the Gabon connection, and Aubameyang is French born of Gabonese heritage, the Black Panther has deeper significance. Wakanda is a fictional African state invented by Marvel Comics and the birthplace of the first black superhero. *Black Panther* has subsequently been made into a very successful film and the Wakanda Forever sign is a symbol of black excellence. Oh, and by the way, Aubameyang has also got a pretty impressive backflip in his locker for other occasions.

What was amusing about the Man in the Mask's magical moment was that Pierre-Emerick had intended to unveil the Wakanda celebration the previous weekend when Arsenal played Manchester United. Everything fell into place when Aubameyang scored a penalty to spark the celebration – but his superhero powers suddenly deserted him as he couldn't find where he'd hidden the mask!

Imitation is the sincerest form of flattery and we only had to wait a couple of weeks for another man-in-a-mask goal celebration. But there was a fundamental flaw in the fun of this one. Wolves striker Raul Jimenez scored his team's second goal in their 2018/19 FA Cup semi-final against Watford at Wembley and immediately ran round to behind the net. He'd placed a wrestling-style mask there and put it on, to the surprise of his team-mates. He'd gone to a lot of trouble with it; the mask was decked out in Wolves' gold and black and included the club badge. WWE enthusiasts clocked it as a Sin Cara mask – as worn by wrestler Jorge Arias (a Mexican, like Jimenez) who fights under that name. The only trouble was Watford responded by pulling one goal back, then another, and went on to clinch a dramatic 3-2 win in extra time. So the Jimenez celebration was not only forgotten about in the excitement that followed but, in retrospect, it looked pretty hollow. The Dutch have a lovely phrase for it: don't sell the skin before you've caught the bear.

Arsenal's Joel Campbell celebrated scoring his first goal at the Emirates, against Sunderland in December 2015, by producing a baby's dummy from down the front of his shorts. He then ran around with it in his mouth – 'for Brianna' he tweeted later. You just wonder how long he'd been keeping the dummy down there – after all, he'd first signed for Arsenal four years earlier. It wasn't the first time a Campbell celebration to do with fatherhood had captured the attention, though his prop this time was already on the field. He scored for Costa Rica against Uruguay in the 2014 World Cup and stuffed the ball under his shirt, cradling it while sucking his thumb. He explained afterwards to Associated Press: 'I'm going to have a son soon, which is why I celebrated my goal the way I did. Celebrating his arrival with a World Cup goal is the best thing that can happen to me.'

The dummy celebration wasn't even original – Carlos Tevez had already been there – and it's probably fair to say the only dummy we want to see on a football pitch is the one a penalty-taker sells to a goalkeeper. The words chicken and Tevez don't really go together but the Argentinian star made his mark early in his long career in professional football with a controversial chicken celebration that landed him in trouble. He scored a crucial goal for Boca Juniors, his first pro club, in a game with big rivals River Plate in 2004 and then went topless so he could better prance around like a demented chicken. Pretty convincing it was, too. The meaning behind it was that Boca fans refer to River Plate players as *gallinas* – or chickens – insinuating that they lack fighting spirit. The referee wasn't without fighting spirit, though, and he sent off Tevez for an inflammatory gesture. And just to show he knew what he was talking about, the official then replicated the chicken celebration with probably slightly too much relish.

Tevez put it all behind him – eventually – to go on to enjoy success with West Ham, both Manchester United and City, and then Juventus. His ongoing celebrations included his own special dance and a little spell when he would also tuck a dummy down his shorts and bring it out if he scored, in honour of his two daughters.

But at least Campbell and Tevez showed a little more restraint than Edmilson Ferreira, a striker with Brazilian club Atletico Mineiro. He celebrated scoring a goal against neighbours America-Belo Horizonte – nicknamed the Rabbits – by pulling a carrot from his shorts and munching on it. Edmilson was spat at by one opponent and hacked down by another, so it's fair to say his rabbit-provoking celebration didn't receive unanimous approval.

Somewhere in a south London lock-up there's probably a box of 4,000 unused red Zorro masks. Charlton fans planned to take them out of their pockets and put them on when their team scored against Fulham in an FA Cup tie on 11 February 2003. But the opportunity never arose to get masked up as they lost the match 3-0, Steed Malbranque scoring a hat-trick. Their idea had been to respond to Fulham striker Facundo Sava, who had pulled a Zorro mask out of his sock and worn it after scoring against Charlton in a previous match. The mask was a trademark celebration for the livewire Sava, and originated when he was playing club football in his native Argentina. Fans of his club Gimnasia y Esgrima La Plata would throw masks on the field after their team had scored. Sava so enjoyed getting involved in their ritual he was sent hundreds of Zorro masks, though he brought just the one with him when he came to England to further his career.

Argentinian international Jonas Gutiérrez joined Newcastle United in 2008 and came with a bit of a reputation as he'd put on a red Spiderman mask after scoring at his previous club, Real Mallorca. But he had to wait so long before scoring that the mask went a bit whiffy stuck down his shorts. He smashed in a goal from 25 yards in a 6-1 defeat of Barnsley and gave St James' Park the chance to see their superhero all masked up. But he told the *Chronicle* in Newcastle: 'I don't know how long the mask has been down there, but it did not smell very nice when I put it on, though I have cleaned it once or twice.' Gutiérrez got the idea of wearing a mask after meeting a young fan in a cinema the night before a game. He explained: 'It all started in Spain. I went to the cinema and a little boy asked me to score a goal for him, so I told him I would put a Spiderman mask on for him as that was his favourite film.'

It was a very different Gutierrez who celebrated a vital goal for Newcastle on the final day of the 2014/15 season. Having already provided the assist for the first in the match against West Ham, he scored the second goal from long range in a 2-0 win to ensure the club's Premier League survival. He whipped off his shirt, brushed off his team-mates and ran to the touchline before cupping his ears towards the directors' box. His defiant gesture was because he was distressed to know it was going to be his last game for Newcastle. It was a miracle he was playing football at all, having been diagnosed with testicular cancer a couple of years earlier and undergone chemotherapy treatment – all of which he had kept private apart from family and very close friends. He later won a disability discrimination lawsuit against Newcastle but continued his football career abroad.

It's not every day your son celebrates his first birthday so Bristol City striker Famara Diedhiou had everything ready in case he scored against Luton on

29 December 2019. It all went perfectly as he raced to the touchline and collected a birthday hat and party popper. From there it didn't go quite so well as he tore the blue paper hat when he tried to cram it on to his head, and the popper just didn't pop when he pulled it. The Senegalese international got it all nicely into proportion after City's 3-0 win when he tweeted: 'When you try to wish a happy first birthday to your son but nothing work and the celebration goes wrong. Doesn't matter – daddy loves you.'

4

Injuries: Breaking the golden rule

THE FIRST rule of goal celebrations is that no one gets hurt. No player should be dropped, punched, gouged or assaulted in the mayhem that follows a golden moment. So, guess what's coming up for your entertainment in this chapter ...

Paulo Diogo broke the rule – and in spectacular fashion during a Swiss First Division match on 5 December 2004 playing for Geneva club Servette away to FC Schaffhausen. And poor old Paulo had nobody to blame but himself. The recently-married midfielder – and his wedding is relevant to what happened next – helped set up an 87th-minute goal for Jean Beausejour. He celebrated by jumping on the metal perimeter fence separating the fans from the pitch. What he didn't anticipate – and this will make you wince – is that as he jumped off again his wedding ring got caught on the fence. And with it, the top part of his finger, which tore off. Ouch. Double Ouch. In an extraordinary twist to an excruciating incident, and while the stewards tried to recover the missing bit of digit for him, Paulo was booked for excessive time-wasting. He was taken to hospital that night but doctors were unable to re-attach the top of his finger. Still, he was able to resume his football career, even going on to play for that day's opponents Schaffhausen. But jumping on any more metal fences was definitely barred forever. And, of course, players are no longer permitted to wear rings.

Every footballer dreads getting injured while celebrating a goal because it turns a golden moment into a stupid one. What's even worse, though, is getting injured while celebrating a goal that's already been disallowed. Step forward Fabian Espindola, an Argentinian playing in the USA's Major League Soccer. He'd already shown off his trademark celebration, a backflip, when he got his first goal for Real Salt Lake. It was when he scored six minutes into a game against Los Angeles Galaxy on 6 September 2008 that adrenalin took over from common sense for Fabian. Out came the backflip and over he went – only to land awkwardly on his ankle and put himself out of the game for eight weeks. And all to no avail, as the goal had already been ruled out for offside. Fighting back tears afterwards, he told the *New York Post*: 'If only I'd seen the offside flag just two seconds sooner, I wouldn't have celebrated and this wouldn't have happened.'

Of all the people who might get injured in the frenzy after England had scored their first goal of a World Cup tournament, a key member of the medical team might have been thought of as the least likely. But physiotherapist Gary Lewin was stretchered off in considerable pain after dislocating his ankle and suffering fractures and ruptured ligaments in a pitch-side accident. Daniel Sturridge had just equalised for England in their opening group match in the 2014 tournament against Italy when Lewin leaped up and landed awkwardly – on a plastic water bottle, according to manager Roy Hodgson. He had to fly home for treatment, but the team, as well as Italy, who went on to win 2-1 that day, soon followed him as they were both surprisingly eliminated from the group.

You can see on YouTube the fraction of a nano-second when Anderson Lopes realises his goal celebration has gone drastically wrong. It could have been fatal, but mercifully it wasn't quite that bad. The Brazilian celebrated his second goal for J-League side Consadore in their 5-2 win over Shimizu S-Pulse in March 2019 by jumping over the advertising hoarding. Although you only see the back view you sense that when he's at the height of his jump he desperately wants to press rewind as he suddenly sees what's behind the hoardings. Not grass, not a running track, not a perimeter path. No, it's a drop of about 15 feet to a concrete concourse. This one has a happy ending as the next thing we see is poor

Anderson, stunned and shocked but still breathing, being helped to his feet. It wasn't as if he'd never been to the ground before as this was a home match for Consadore, but as it was the opening game of the season in the Japanese league perhaps Anderson didn't know his surroundings as well as he might. Bet he never tried that celebration again, though.

Another player who hurt himself celebrating a goal missed almost a whole season with the injury. Nicolai Muller got the only goal of the game for Hamburger SV against Augsburg in August 2017 but fell to the ground in agony following an over-the-top jumping celebration. He suffered an anterior cruciate ligament injury and had to be taken off, only returning to football in the penultimate game of that German league season.

Argentinian striker Martin Palermo did many good things in his career, but he'll go down in history as the man who missed three penalties all in the one game, as well as breaking his leg when a wall fell on him as he celebrated a goal. He was playing in Spain for Villarreal and went to celebrate with the fans behind the goal after scoring against Levante in extra time in a cup tie. But a concrete wall collapsing shattered his leg and put him out of action and meant he missed the opportunity to play in the 2002 World Cup.

It wasn't even his goal, but Shaun Goater was so thrilled when Manchester City scored through Nicolas Anelka late in a game at Birmingham in

October 2002 to clinch a 2-0 win that he kicked an advertising hoarding and had to be substituted because of an injured knee. Apparently, the one and only Kevin Keegan, City's manager at the time, wasn't too pleased with the man known as The Goat.

Twitter nowadays allows players to explain first-hand the reason for their celebration. Or, in the case of Michy Batshuayi, what it felt like when his celebration went painfully wrong. When Belgian team-mate Adnan Januzaj scored the only goal of the game in a 1-0 win over England in the 2018 World Cup, the Chelsea striker decided to celebrate by grabbing the ball and kicking it with all his might. Unfortunately for him, that was about four yards before the ball hit the goalpost and rebounded slap into his face. Batshuayi showed a nice line in not taking himself too seriously by explaining on Twitter: 'Fortnite celebrations so overrated so I had to create something new. Why am I so stupid, bro?' It took more than a year but Chelsea keeper Kepa Arrizabalaga joined Batshuayi in the embarrassing ball-in-the-face club when a shot from an Ajax player in a Champions League match in November 2019 hit the post and rebounded into his face and then into the goal. Poor Kepa was credited with an own goal and then got an amusingly unsympathetic tweet from Batshuayi: 'Welcome to the memes club, bro.'

Veteran goalkeeper Gianluigi Buffon celebrated Italy's 2-0 win over Belgium in Euro 2016 by running the length of the pitch, jumping on to the crossbar and swinging on it. And then falling off. The Juventus player later admitted the fall had hurt, but he didn't want to show it and jumped straight up to celebrate with the joyous Italian fans. Buffon was 38 at the time. Old enough to know better? Possibly, but who's going to tell him?

It comes to something when an invading fan injures a player but that's what happened to Liverpool goalkeeper Adrian as he celebrated winning the UEFA Super Cup in August 2019. He'd just saved the crucial Chelsea penalty in a shoot-out and was enjoying himself with his Liverpool team-mates when the fan came on and slipped as he tried to invade the fun and fell on Adrian's ankle. Not a serious injury, but undoubtedly painful and annoying nevertheless.

No player likes being dropped and certainly it's not a word to be used around Arsenal defender Steve Morrow. His captain Tony Adams attempted to pick Morrow up after the Gunners had won the 1993 League Cup Final against Sheffield Wednesday, a match in which Morrow had scored the winning goal. But Adams slipped and dropped his team-mate, meaning unlucky Morrow missed the medal presentations and was ruled out of the rest of the season with a broken arm. That cost him the chance of playing in an FA Cup Final as Arsenal went on to complete a cup double by beating poor old Sheffield Wednesday in that final, too. Before the second match, Morrow, his arm in a sling, was belatedly presented with his League Cup winners' medal.

What is it about Arsenal, as star striker Thierry Henry, who's normally super cool, went to celebrate scoring the winning goal against Chelsea on 6 May 2000? He hit himself in the face with the corner flag when it snapped as he pretended to use it as a mic stand for an Elvis impression! He had to have medical attention before resuming the game. What was it Oscar Wilde said about something going wrong once is a misfortune but if it happens twice it looks like carelessness? Well, later in his career, in the United States, Thierry did just that when he scored a great goal for New York Red Bulls to give them a 1-0 win over New England Revolution. He kicked the corner flag as part of his celebration only to break it in half. Incidentally, and not a corner flag is mentioned in this story, Henry once explained what another of his celebrations meant, having scored for Arsenal against Liverpool in 2006. He ran around smelling his fingers, saying he did it because he'd sniffed out an error from Steven Gerrard.

And returning momentarily to unnecessary injuries and Arsenal, Henry's ex-team-mate Perry Groves was on the bench for another match when his team scored and he jumped up to celebrate, only to hit his head on the dug-out roof. He knocked himself out and needed treatment from the physio.

Footballers, eh?

5

Women's football:
That's the tea

EVERY WHICH way, the United States dominated the 2019 Women's World Cup. They comfortably won the competition, retaining the trophy they had also collected four years earlier, and took first place in the celebrations controversies as well.

Captain Megan Rapinoe sparked one debate with her rather superior posing, there was a row over what was alleged to be disrespectful over-celebrating in a one-sided group game, and top scorer Alex Morgan capped them with her ironic tea-sipping gesture after scoring against England in the semi-final.

First of all, Rapinoe, who celebrated goals during the tournament with an arched-back smug-smiled Cantona-like pose. Her response to accusations of arrogance was refreshingly unapologetic. 'Wah, wah, wah,' she replied when challenged. 'We're at the World Cup, what do you want us to do? This is the biggest stage, the biggest moment. We work hard, we like to play hard and we like to have fun and enjoy ourselves.'

This followed a row in the first week of the tournament as the USA team celebrated each and every one of their goals in a record-breaking 13-0 group stage victory against luckless Thailand. Criticism came from rival countries where the ongoing celebrations were described as unnecessary and disrespectful. Former Canadian international Kaylyn Kyle claimed it was disgraceful but then had to endure death threats on social media for her strong views. USA head coach Jill Ellis fiercely defended her team, saying any disrespect would have come only if they'd taken it easy on Thailand and stopped trying to score against them. Captain Rapinoe, who later that summer was named FIFA World Player of the Year, weighed in: 'I think our only crime was an explosion of joy. If our crime is joy, then we'll take that.' Thailand coach Nuengrutai Srathongvian graciously said she took no offence at the celebrations, simply insisting that her side had to improve.

And then there was birthday girl Alex Morgan's tea-drinking celebration after heading her team's second goal in a 2-1 semi-final win over England. There's no doubt she meant it, cocking her little finger to emphasise the tea-sipping image (which is apparently what the world thinks we do with our pinky). But debate raged over what she actually meant by it. Was it just a simple mickey-take of the

English and our love for a cuppa? Or was it something altogether more significant, and a reference to the Boston Tea Party? That was the important game-changer in 1773 when tea was thrown in the sea off Boston, setting in motion American independence from British rule. Out in the US, *Time* magazine claimed Morgan was responsible for some 'masterful trolling' and the 'ultimate power move' against a nation that loves its tea almost as much as it used to love colonising. Morgan denied both theories, explaining that the expression 'that's the tea' means 'that's the situation' and the situation was she had scored and the US were in the final. She expanded later: 'I feel like this team has had so much thrown at them. I feel like we didn't take an easy route through this tournament and "that's the tea".'

Celebrations being such a part of the game nowadays, it wasn't only the good old US of A who commanded attention at the 2019 Women's World Cup. Norway had set a pretty good standard on the second day of the tournament when they beat Nigeria 3-0. Lisa-Marie Utland blasted home the second goal, smashing her shot through the keeper's hands, and the Norway team celebrated together by pretending to take a selfie. The imaginary camera was held by goal-creator Guro Reiten as all the girls smiled and gurned and posed behind her as if she was really taking their picture for posterity.

Canada also went for the pre-planned all-in-it-together celebration when a far post header by

Kadeisha Buchanan from a corner gave them the only goal of the game in their opening match against Cameroon. Theirs was a nicely-executed basketball take-off with Kadeisha given the honour of scoring the pretend basket while her team-mates swarmed round for a hand-slap each.

Scotland striker Erin Cuthbert had it all planned for her celebration, and got the chance after scoring in an exciting 3-3 draw with Argentina in a group game. She kissed a picture of herself as a youngster, the photo having been given to her by her father to remind her it was her younger self she was playing for when she went out to represent her country.

England's top scorer Ellen White created the chance time and time again to unveil a personal celebration, aimed at her husband in the stand. She always pretended to put on goggles because she and 'Mr White' once liked a similar celebration by Cologne striker Anthony Modeste while they were watching a match in the German Bundesliga together. Nice touch, but pretend goggles aren't quite as romantic as a Gareth Bale love-heart.

Team-mate Nikita Parris, meanwhile, set off at full speed after scoring, shouting, thumping her badge, and trying to avoid all her team-mates as she sprinted to celebrate in front of the team bench. Once there, she put four fingers in front of her face while waving her hand, a gesture to her close friends in the England squad who had named themselves the four musketeers. Sorry, Nikita, you'll have to drop someone from your gang as the novel was called *The Three Musketeers*.

The USA have form for provocation and New Zealand's women's team manager Tony Readings told us in no uncertain terms how it felt for him after his side had lost to America in the quarter-finals of the 2012 Olympics. The US team did cartwheels after scoring on their way to a 2-0 win as a tribute to their country's Olympic gold-medal-winning gymnastic squad. In previous rounds they'd held up a piece of paper wishing an absent team-mate a happy birthday, as well as performing 'the worm' – all the players stand in a line and hold hands, wiggling them in turn in the air, to look like … a worm. Defeated manager Readings was furious. 'I wouldn't like it if our team did that,' he told the media. 'When teams concede a goal they want to get on with the game. It's obviously something the Americans work on in training. We try to work on scoring goals, we haven't got time to work on celebrations.'

US coach Pia Sundhage, also known for singing Simon and Garfunkel songs during press conferences, didn't attempt to bridge the troubled waters and said: 'We score goals and you're happy. If the players come up with ideas, that's perfectly fine.' Controversial celebrants or not, the US team had obviously practised their moves in more ways than one as they went on to win Olympic gold, beating Japan 2-1 in the final at Wembley.

Rumour has it there are far more salacious sights on the internet than Brandi Chastain whipping off her shirt to celebrate winning the Women's World Cup. It was more chaste Chastain than anything, but the world – well America anyway – went mad for it. Brandi's image was plastered everywhere and it transformed her life. She subsequently got to appear naked in a magazine, with suitably covered-up bits, star in reality TV shows, write a book, and work as a football commentator.

Chastain had been a regular in the USA women's soccer team when they battled their way through to the World Cup finals in 1999. She'd already won an Olympic gold medal but as the World Cup was being staged in her home state of California this was always going to be the crowning moment of her career. The final against China was held on 10 July at the Rose Bowl in Pasadena and had the biggest crowd at a women's sports event in history, with an official attendance of 90,185. Among them was US President Bill Clinton and he watched two world super states battle out a goalless draw, even after extra time. So it went to penalties.

It was all down to the fifth one and when Brandi left-footed it into the corner to win the cup, she understandably lost her mind. And her shirt. Off it came and Brandi, now wearing only a black sports bra on her top half, sunk to her knees in delight. 'Momentary insanity' was how she explained it: 'I wasn't thinking about anything.' Brandi might not have been thinking of much at that moment – but her publicity department certainly was.

A few years later and one celebration that didn't go down too well with the boss came from Kelly Smith when she scored twice for England in a 2007 World Cup match with Japan. Star striker Kelly took off her Umbro boot – nice touch for them – and kissed it. But England manager Hope Powell had words with her afterwards. For two reasons. One, it created more attention for Kelly herself, and the manager thought she could end up being more targeted by the opposition than even she was used to. Two, Powell found the celebration a tad disrespectful.

No, Hope. If we're going to worry about stopping celebrations because the opposition might find them disrespectful, then we won't have a book packed full of them.

6

Strikers: A Law unto themselves

LET'S FOCUS now on the main man: the striker. The one who knows which way to run when a goal's been scored, who to thank, and exactly what to do for a celebration.

We'll start by having a quick look at how some of our absolute favourite goalscorers over the years would typically celebrate their goals:

Gary Lineker – both arms raised high, huge grin, head slightly down, sprint towards his nearest colleagues. Jimmy Greaves – occasionally seen with one arm outstretched upwards, but mostly just a walk away to leave his team-mates doing the bouncing around. George Best – invariably just his right arm going straight up, often with a little punch of the air but usually with a sort of hint of embarrassment at how good he was. Michael Owen – usually both arms though sometimes just the one, and normally heading for the fans behind the goal. Kevin Keegan – a little jump in the air often followed by a leap into a colleague's arms and when he's up there a punch towards the sky with his right fist. Kenny Dalglish – a quick turn away from the goal with arms already aloft and a beaming smile across his face. Gianfranco Zola – both arms stretched horizontally, and off to celebrate in front of the nearest fans. Trevor Francis – one arm in the air, but both if it was a very important goal or a very good one. Mark Hughes – usually just a one-arm salute, but always a very quick sprint away from the action. Jermain Defoe – says his celebrations are influenced by Ian Wright, and they consist of both arms stretched out straight. Ian Rush – arms up in the air and a running jump into the arms of the nearest team-mate.

There's a statue outside Old Trafford to prove Denis Law is a Manchester United legend. And before it was even fashionable, he had a trademark celebration – right arm raised straight up, clutching his cuff, and pointing his index finger to the sky. But when the man known as the King scored in the Manchester derby for City against United on 27 April 1974 there was no sign of it. In fact, Law was stony-faced, he'd have put his hands in his pockets if he could, and he looked even more miserable when grinning City team-mates came up to congratulate him.

The Scotland international had previously enjoyed an illustrious career on the red side of Manchester, winning the *Ballon d'Or* award and a couple of league championships, though a knee injury cost him his place in the 1968 European Cup triumph. He switched to City for what turned out to be his final season of professional football, 1973/74 – after all, he didn't have to move house to play for them. As chance would have it, the Manchester derby was the penultimate game that season and United went into it deep in the relegation mire. With ten minutes to go, it was still goalless when Law, lurking as ever in the area looking for that moment of opportunity, picked up a loose ball while still sideways on to the goal. That didn't stop him, and he casually backheeled the ball into the net. 1-0, and with the other results going against them, it spelled relegation for United. Even though the match was abandoned because of pitch invasions, the result stood.

Law looked mortified at what he'd done to his old club, and years later he still regretted what had happened in what turned out to be his last ever game. United obviously didn't hold it against him, though, as he's centre stage in a statue unveiled in 2008 outside Old Trafford with George Best on one side of him and Bobby Charlton on the other. And that's pretty good company to keep.

A magical goal scored for Arsenal at Newcastle in 2002 by Dennis Bergkamp was voted the best goal in the first 20 seasons of the Premier League. A BBC poll attracted more than half a million votes and more than a third of them were for the Bergkamp masterpiece. The goal came when Robert Pires crossed from the left in to Bergkamp, who was tightly marked with his back to the goal. But he flicked the ball first time past the defender, ran round him the other way, and placed it past Shay Given in the Newcastle goal. The Dutchman's celebration was typically restrained. He did a high five with a team-mate and clenched his fist, which was always Bergkamp's instinctive reaction to one of his many goals. And he looked moderately satisfied with what he'd done.

Never mind that he was the striker who played all seven games for his country in the World Cup finals and didn't score in any one of them, Olivier Giroud has the winner's medal to prove that he was a key player for France in the 2018 competition. He's had an illustrious career, much of it in England, and will always be remembered for the astonishing goal he scored for Arsenal against Crystal Palace on New Year's Day in 2017. A cross came in from the left slightly behind him, with Giroud still running at top speed. He can't have been able to actually see what he was doing but he stuck his left foot out full stretch behind him and somehow contrived to volley it into the top corner off the bar. It was immediately nicknamed the 'scorpion kick' and won him the prestigious FIFA Puskas Award for goal of the year 2017. As he got his wonder goal on 1 January, all his rivals had 364 days to do something better and not one of them managed it.

Giroud modestly accepted the honour at a ceremony at the London Palladium and said: 'I'd just like to thank the people who voted for me, I would like to thank my team-mates, as without them I couldn't have scored this goal, and my family.' Arsenal manager Arsene Wenger was a little more loquacious: 'He transformed that goal into art. It was art because of the surprise, because of the beauty of the movement and because of the efficiency of the movement.'

Fast forward to the next match after the Palace fun and games, just two days later, and obviously Giroud had it up his sleeve to remind Arsenal fans of his moment of instinctive genius and pure glory. But it all went wrong in the match at Bournemouth as the home side scored one, then two, and then a third, leaving Giroud not much more to do than take the restarts. Then came the fightback and Arsenal were already back to 3-2 when Bournemouth had a player harshly sent off. More Gunners pressure and Giroud headed the equaliser from close range with two minutes of added time already played. And he celebrated. Racing to the Arsenal fans he re-enacted his scorpion pose, though some unkindly thought it reminded them more of the 'Bring Me Sunshine' closing sequence of a Morecambe and Wise show. But while he was prancing, some of his team-mates were dying to get on with the game. The momentum was all with Arsenal at that point and playing 11 v 10 they fancied nicking the winner. A nice celebration, but not one for cutting into what precious time was left.

Some people might claim that Wayne Rooney didn't get everything right during a long and record-breaking career in English football. But he certainly did when he took just the opposite approach to Giroud a couple of weeks later after scoring an injury-time equaliser for Manchester United as a substitute away to Stoke. It was a pretty special goal, too, a swerving and powerful free kick from way out on the left wing, made even more special as it broke the legendary Bobby Charlton's goalscoring record for Manchester United, which stood at 249 and had been in existence for 44 years. But as the ball whistled in, records were furthest from Rooney's mind. He pointed at the ball in the back of the Stoke net, brushed aside his colleagues, and ran to his own half to try to plot an unlikely winning goal. He didn't make it, but after the match he graciously accepted the many congratulations on his record achievement. Classy.

Sadio Mane 'did a Rooney' when Liverpool got a late equaliser at Manchester United on 19 October 2019. While team-mates congratulated substitute Adam Lallana on his first goal for more than two years, Mane can be seen urging them back towards the centre circle. This Is Anfield tweeted: 'Sadio Mane dragging the players back on when celebrating Lallana's equaliser. There was a game to be won. Top attitude.' Sadio's intervention was to no avail as the game ended 1-1.

Another player criticised for what was reckoned to be an inappropriate celebration was Aston Villa's Ahmed Elmohamady, who scored against Liverpool in the Carabao Cup in 2019 when his shot deflected in off an opponent. The Egyptian defender took his vigorous arms-stretched celebration seriously but Liverpool fans raced to social media to have a go at him as their over-worked club had rested all their first team and fielded a very young side instead. One of the critics commented: 'Divock Origi scored the goal that won us the Champions League and walked to the corner flag. Elmohamady scored a deflected shot against Liverpool Under-18s and went over the top with his celebration.' Incidentally, when he was playing for Hull in 2014, Elmohamady followed a trend at the time of borrowing a remote-controlled camera left behind the goal by a photographer to take some selfies of him and his celebrating mates. The occasion was an FA Cup semi-final at Wembley after Hull had just knocked out Yorkshire rivals Sheffield United.

There's no YouTube clip of this prolific goalscorer celebrating a hat-trick in an FA Cup tie in 1974, but I saw it for myself so you'll have to take my word for it. The match in question was a first round replay between Cambridge United and Hitchin Town. As a Football League club at home to non-league opposition, Cambridge were clear favourites and they duly won 3-0. Nigel Cassidy, an old-fashioned striker who had been brought to the club to score goals, had been having a lean time but got all three this day against opponents from the Isthmian League. But, for my taste, he celebrated too extravagantly, rushing around in delight as if he'd won the FA

Cup itself. Full-time pros should always beat part-timers, and show a bit of humility in the process. A beaming smile, a gracious nod, that's all it would have taken. Sad to say, Cassidy, who was clearly a decent and popular man, is no longer with us. He moved to Cornwall and became a publican, in the time-honoured way that footballers used to do, but died in 2008 after a short illness.

A Premier League team knocking a Championship side out of the FA Cup isn't quite the same as professionals beating semi-pros, but Glenn Murray got it spot on when Brighton beat Millwall in the quarter-final of the competition in March 2019. It had been quite a battle, with Millwall – who were involved in a relegation struggle at the time – leading 2-0 before Brighton levelled the tie with two goals in the last few minutes. After extra time was inconclusive, Millwall led in the penalty shoot-out as well, before crashing out in sudden death. When Millwall missed the decisive spot-kick, all the Brighton players raced towards the penalty area to celebrate with the now mandatory pile-on. Except Murray. Instead, he just turned to the distraught Millwall players and began going along their line, congratulating them one by one. Dignified and respectful, it was a lovely gesture. And as the experienced Murray probably appreciated, you don't get any medals for winning a quarter-final.

We all have a second favourite team, and for many it's Southampton – even when they had that funny out-of-character period when they were signing internationals like Kevin Keegan, Peter Shilton, Charlie George, and others. And if Southampton's a second favourite team, then one of their best ever players was probably a second favourite player for many. Mick Channon. A club stalwart with over 500 appearances for the Saints, and possessor of a famous celebration at a time when celebrations weren't even famous at all.

It was so good it even had its own name. The Windmill. With a broad grin across his ever-happy face, Channon ran away after scoring, with his right arm whirling. It was an unrestrained and hopefully unplanned expression of pure joy and satisfaction. Channon, who went on to become a successful racehorse trainer after his football career, scored more than 200 windmill-celebrated goals for his local club Southampton, and played nearly 50 times for England during the 1970s. His celebration had a lot in common with The Who's Pete Townshend while playing his guitar. Wonder Who got there first?

Runner-up to thumb-sucking as the most annoying of celebrations is a player putting a hand across his mouth and smirking at opposition fans with a sort of look-what-I've-just-done pose. But it wasn't like that when Scotland international Jason Cummings scored twice in 15 minutes after coming on as a substitute for Shrewsbury to earn them a 2-2 draw in an FA Cup fourth round tie with Liverpool on 26 January 2020. Cummings has got what it's fair to call copious tattoos and one of them is a smile on the back of his hand. It's like a clown's, with big red lips and shiny white teeth and just to make sure we know what's going on it has the word Smile tattooed underneath. So when he scored, Cummings clamped the hand across his mouth, with his thumb one side of his nose and his fingers on the others, so the tattoo smile was superimposed over his actual mouth. Clever, eh? Cummings is known in football as a bit of a card – just to prove it, he's got the Joker tattooed on his thigh – and his team-mates were laughing all the way back to the home dressing room at the chance of playing at Anfield in a replay against the reigning world and European champions.

A prolific goalscorer in a career with several different clubs, Michael Chopra's main claim to fame is that he became the first player of Indian parentage to play and score in the Premier League. He also showed a flair for a nice line in goal celebration, whipping off his boot after putting one in for Cardiff against Bristol City and pretending to have his fingers burnt when he went to touch it. His manager at the time, Dave Jones, commented succinctly: 'Chopra is on fire at the moment.'

Well over 20 years after it was first dramatically revealed in England, you can still see Fabrizio Ravanelli's celebration in many a playground or playing field. It's iconic. The enigmatic Italian, known as the White Feather for his distinctive hair, would always lift his shirt up and over his eyes after scoring. With arms outstretched, he'd then run around, six-pack stomach prominently on display. Few who saw his Premier League debut for Middlesbrough after he joined the club for a record fee from Juventus in 1996 will forget it. He scored a hat-trick in a thrilling 3-3 draw with Liverpool and out came that trademark move. Middlesbrough fans honoured him to the tune of an old standard, 'That's Amore': 'When the White Feather scores, you can hear Boro roar ... Ravanelli.'

Talking of fans serenading players when they score, Malcolm Macdonald loved it when the Newcastle fans sang 'Supermac, Superstar, how many goals have you scored so far' (to the tune of 'Jesus Chris Superstar') when he scored a hat-trick on his home debut for the club. That was back in 1971, and he said he's often wondered how supporters seemed to spontaneously know the words as if they'd all been given song-sheets at the turnstiles. One celebration ritual at the time, as Supermac recalled in a later interview with the Newcastle *Chronicle*, was that manager Joe Harvey would light up a cigarette for him as he entered the dressing room afterwards if he'd had a good match. Don't think that particular custom has survived ...

I was at Wembley on 16 April 1975 when Macdonald scored all five England goals in a European Championship qualifier against Cyprus. If memory serves me right he celebrated earnestly by raising both arms towards the night sky.

It might be mayhem all round him, with players jumping up and down and sliding about, and the yellow wall behind the goal going mad, but striker

Erling Haaland remains the calmest man around. His goal celebration is to sit on the ground with legs crossed in the Lotus meditation position – a move once displayed by Mo Salah at Liverpool as well. Haaland was born in Leeds in 2000, where his dad Alf-Inge was playing at the time, but moved to Norway when he was a lad. Before he was 20 he'd played in the Champions League for both Red Bull Salzburg and Borussia Dortmund. The German club boasts the biggest stadium in the country and the yellow wall is the largest free-standing grandstand in Europe. Meditate on that …

Not for Dominic Calvert-Lewin a predictable knee-slide or corner flag jig – he chose a lawnmower celebration as his trademark move after scoring for Everton. He promised on Sky Sports' *Soccer AM* in 2017 he would use that as his celebration the next time he scored, and was as good as his word. It involved pretending to yank up the starter cord and then as it revs up, pushing the lawnmower forward with both hands. And he was still doing it a couple of years later – Calvert-Lewin loves that move, even if it's not clear if anyone else does.

In a game probably best remembered for Gary Lineker being substituted in the second half of his final match for England, and then the next day for a national newspaper coming up with the headline 'Swedes 2 Turnips 1', there was also a terrific goal and a pretty special celebration. England were leading Sweden 1-0 in Euro 92, needing a win to ensure progression to the semi-finals, but conceded two in the second half to go out of the competition. The winner was scored by Thomas Brolin, who unleashed his trademark pirouette celebration, jumping up – very high – and twisting around with his arm raised to the sky. It was a career highlight for Brolin, who had a meteoric rise in the football world but left just as quickly, retiring at 29 after playing as a substitute goalkeeper in his final professional game.

Graziano Pelle is a big rugby fan and two of his celebrations after scoring for Southampton in 2015 showed his love for the game. After scoring against Manchester United he grabbed a pretend rugby ball, dived over a pretend try-line, and scored a pretend try. A few weeks later the Italian striker scored against Bournemouth and this time he did a version of the haka, the New Zealand rugby dance, with the club's Kiwi-born sports therapist.

Harry Kane has scored all those goals for Spurs and England but perhaps his most memorable celebration came in a match he wasn't even playing in. It was at the end of the Champions League semi-final in Amsterdam on 8 May 2019 when Spurs had fought back from two-down at half-time to win 3-2 against Ajax thanks to a Lucas Moura hat-trick. Kane had been out injured for a month after hurting his ankle in the quarter-final when Spurs knocked out Premier League champions Manchester City. The sight of Kane running at full pelt to join in the semi-final celebrations was a huge boost for Spurs and the club's fans, with the hope it demonstrated he would be fit to play in the final against Liverpool in just under four weeks' time. He was, but the story doesn't have a happy ending as Kane played but Spurs lost the game 2-0.

Kane loves scoring but he's not big on goal celebrations. There's always a huge smile on his face whether he's netted for club or country, but apart from that he's pretty restrained. Sometimes he'll run away with both arms outstretched, at other times he'll put an arm up and point skywards, and he's also been known to kiss his wedding ring finger. His wife Kate responded to the latter with a picture of them together posted on Instagram accompanied by a love-heart. How sweet.

It's ironic that one of the best goals ever scored in the FA Cup should have changed the life not of the player who scored it, but of the man who was commentating on it for the BBC. Non-league Hereford United were at home to mighty Newcastle United in the third round of the competition on 5 February 1972. Hereford's Ronnie Radford won the ball back for his team with a ferocious tackle in midfield and played a one-two with a colleague in a more advanced position. The return pass bobbled up nicely on a mudheap of a pitch and Radford lashed it home first time from fully 30 yards. Whatever he had planned for a celebration didn't last long as it sparked a pitch invasion of hundreds of home fans, and Radford disappeared from view. But not before his excited sprint with arms aloft had meant his shirt rode up and exposed a bare midriff – that simply wouldn't happen to the image-conscious modern-day footballer.

Up in the commentary box, a young John Motson, at the very start of his career, described the moment in beautifully passionate detail. It took a whole lot more hard graft, but his illustrious BBC career certainly took off from that moment. Right place, right time. After all, it's a goal and a commentary that has been replayed almost as many times as there have been goals scored in the FA Cup.

Hereford won the match 2-1, becoming the lowest-ranked non-league side to beat a top-flight opponent in English footballing history. And two days later, Radford was back in his day job, working as a joiner on a building site. Much later, he lovingly recalled the details of that day for a BBC interview, saying: 'People still talk about it with such enthusiasm. A fan once told me that a Japanese businessman asked him where he was from. When he said Hereford, the Japanese guy replied: "Aaah, giant-killers! Do you know Ronnie Radford?"!'

7

Politics: Crossing the line

CUPPING BOTH ears is a pretty familiar goal celebration as players run towards whoever's been abusing them with a gesture of 'What do you say now?' or 'I've heard it all before.' We've seen both David Beckham and Jamie Vardy put their hands behind their ears towards opposition fans who'd been taunting them with provocatively rude chants about their celebrity wives.

For Raheem Sterling the gesture was altogether more meaningful after he'd scored England's fifth goal in a qualifier in Montenegro for the 2020 European Championship. Sterling ran towards home supporters in Podgorica and cupped his ears, responding to what had been disgraceful racist barracking. He won great acclaim for his bravery that night, and taking on the abusive fans with his gesture. It wasn't the first time that season he'd been subjected to racial taunts, a couple of Chelsea supporters abusing him while he was playing for Manchester City earlier in the season. Sterling maintains he's not trying to become a spokesman for any anti-racism campaign but at the same time he won't back down from confronting it. He pointedly turned his back on the racist fans in Montenegro to greet his team-mates and said afterwards: 'It wasn't an outpouring of frustration. It was just to let them know that you're going to have to do better than that to stop us.'

That was the attitude of all the England players when they were subjected to horrifying and concerted racial abuse in Sofia as they hammered Bulgaria 6-0 in another European Championship qualifier in October 2019. Sterling was again among the goals as England players preferred to confront the abuse by inflicting a big defeat on the home nation, rather than the option of walking off. He tweeted afterwards: 'Feeling sorry for Bulgaria to be represented by such idiots in their stadium.'

Another unforgiveable case of racial abuse occurred in Italy and Sterling again weighed in with a dignified and swift contribution. It came after 19-year-old Juventus player Moise Kean was subjected to monkey chants by Cagliari fans after scoring against them in April 2019. One of his team-mates, Leonardo Bonucci, criticised Kean for his celebration, which consisted of standing with his arms outstretched and staring the fans out. 'He shouldn't have done that and the fans shouldn't have reacted that way. We have to set the example and not provoke anyone.' The Juventus manager also had a go at Kean but, to be fair to Bonucci, he later backed down from his incredible first assessment, saying he had been misunderstood and he condemned all forms of racism and discrimination. Sterling had added to the debate by poking fun at Bonucci's 50-50 attribution of blame – he may not want to be in the forefront of the campaign against racist behaviour, but he certainly assumed a leading role.

And while we've got a serious head on, everyone knows politics and football don't mix, but the draw for the 2018 World Cup finals provided a temptation that was just too much to resist. The match in question was between Switzerland and Serbia with both teams going into it with a great chance of qualifying for the last 16 of the tournament. As fate would have it, two of the players in the Swiss team – Xherdan Shaqiri and Granit Xhaka – were of Kosovan descent and they both scored in a dramatic, hard-fought 2-1 win. Kosovo and Serbia have been bitter foes since the break-up of Yugoslavia began in the early 1990s. Both Xhaka and Shaqiri's families are from Kosovo, where a Serbian crackdown on the Albanian population ended with NATO military intervention in 1999. The antagonism has never gone away and there were jeers and boos by Serbian fans from the moment the Swiss players' names were read out over the PA. In a tense atmosphere on and off the field, Xhaka equalised for his adopted country after Serbia went ahead and then Shaqiri ran from the halfway line to score the winner in the 90th minute. Both goalscorers celebrated with an Albanian eagle gesture, a nationalist symbol representing the double-headed eagle on the country's national flag.

Of course, Serbian fans reacted to the provocation and politicians subsequently weighed in on both sides to have their say on the controversy. Shaqiri downplayed it all afterwards, saying it was just emotion at scoring the winning goal, but his boots have for a long time had a Swiss flag on one and a Kosovan flag on the other to demonstrate his dual loyalties. The Swiss team manager Vladimir Petkovic, himself Bosnia-born, said at the time: 'It's clear that emotions show up but we need to stay away from politics in football and we should focus on this sport as a beautiful game and something that brings people together.'

Both Shaqiri and Xhaka were subsequently fined for their actions by FIFA but escaped suspensions, which had been mooted as a possibility.

We need to stay away from politics in football, the man said, but either Alejandro Bedoya hadn't heard the advice, or decided to ignore it anyway. He scored for Philadelphia Union against DC United in the USA on 4 August 2019, and after celebrating with his mates, ran to find one of the TV company's microphones at the side of the pitch. The team's captain, he knelt and shouted the message on live television: 'Congress, do something now. End gun violence.' Bedoya had previously expressed on Twitter his opinions on gun laws and he said after the game:

'It was spur of the moment. A call to action. Words can mean a lot, and hopefully this continues the conversation and leads to action.' Powerful and topical words and if the jury's out on whether the time and place were wisely chosen, good for Alejandro for getting his opinions out there.

Paul Pogba is one of the great entertainers with his goal celebrations but when he scored for Manchester United against Newcastle in a 4-1 win on 18 November 2017, his focus was altogether more serious. He put his wrists together, dedicating the celebration to Libyan people. 'My prayers go to those suffering slavery in Libya. May Allah be by your side and may this cruelty come to an end,' he posted on Instagram.

There was nothing political about it, said Didier Drogba, after he faced criticism from Turkish football authorities for revealing a t-shirt saying 'Thank You Madiba' under his Galatasaray kit. It was just after Madiba – South African hero Nelson Mandela – had died, in December 2013, and he was someone former Chelsea striker Drogba had actually met and spent time with. Drogba commented: 'I am sorry but I would do the same if the same thing happened again. I didn't do this for political reason. I did this because Mandela not only inspired me but a country, a continent and the world. Thank you again, Madiba.'

During a hugely successful career at Chelsea, and always with a delighted look on his face at the sheer pleasure of scoring, Drogba was a great celebrator of all the 100-plus goals he scored for them. He's most remembered for sliding on his knees towards the fans, with his back arched and his fists pumping. But at various times, he's also offered up salutes, laid flat on his back, pointed at the sky, spun the corner flag around and ran bare-chested while waving his shirt. And he's also kept an eye on how players following in his footsteps have copied his moves. He praised Chelsea striker Tammy Abraham and Arsenal's Pierre-Emerick Aubameyang for copying his knee slide, captioning a photo on Instagram of Aubameyang with 'When your lil bro does your signature.'

But back to politics and Egyptian midfielder Mohamed Aboutrika revealed a t-shirt with the message 'Sympathy for Gaza' after scoring against Sudan in the 2008 African Cup of Nations. He was given a yellow card for displaying a political slogan.

One-club man Carles Puyol played nearly 600 games for Barcelona and more than 100 for Spain but will also be remembered for a political gesture he made in celebration of a goal. A Barcelona side managed by Pep Guardiola won 6-2 away to massive rivals Real Madrid on 2 May 2009, and it was defender and captain Puyol who got the crucial second goal. He celebrated by taking off his captain's armband, kissing it and holding it aloft for all the ground to see. The armband is in the colours of the Catalan flag and therefore a powerful symbol of those campaigning for Catalonia to have its independence from Spain. Puyol said after retiring from the game that he'd lived the dream of every Catalan child by playing for Barcelona.

Any book on football celebrations homes in on the joyous, the funny, the clever, but it must also acknowledge that occasionally players have crossed a line. Way across the line in the case of France international striker Nicolas Anelka. He was penalised by the Football Association with a five-match suspension, fined £80,000, and ordered to complete an education course, after an offensive racist gesture while playing for West Bromwich Albion against West Ham on 28 December 2013. His offence was a quenelle gesture, though Anelka defended himself by claiming he intended it to be seen as anti-establishment as opposed to anti-Semitic.

Another player with outrageous talent and equally outrageous views was Paolo Di Canio, who was fined and suspended in 2005 for making a fascist salute while playing in Italy for Lazio. Not that Di Canio, notorious in his career in England for pushing over a referee and getting an 11-match ban from playing for Sheffield Wednesday, had kept his political opinions private. He has called Italian dictator Mussolini 'basically a very principled, ethical individual' who was 'deeply misunderstood'. He was later suspended from his role as a Sky Italia pundit after showing on air his tattoo of the word 'dux' which also refers to Mussolini.

A celebration which looked suspiciously like something else was the one by Ezgjan Alioski in Leeds United's 2-0 win over local rivals Huddersfield in December 2019. With his left hand horizontal across his upper lip and his right arm pointing across the pitch it looked very much like a Nazi salute. Not so, Alioski told Sky Sports after the match. He was merely pointing at the club's general manager, Matt Grice, who had grown a moustache for the Movember charity. 'It was a celebration for him, not a gesture for other things,' said the Macedonian international. Nothing to see here.

And then there was the political slogan Robbie Fowler revealed during a colourful career when he lifted up his Liverpool shirt after scoring his second goal in his team's 3-0 European Cup Winners' Cup win over Brann Bergen of Norway in March 1997. His t-shirt underneath declared support for sacked Liverpool dockers who were involved in a bitter dispute at the time.

UEFA fined him 2,000 Swiss francs, pointing out a football ground is not the right stage for political demonstrations.

Ironically, just two days earlier, Fowler had received a pat on the back from FIFA after questioning the award of a penalty in his favour after he appeared to be brought down by Arsenal goalkeeper David Seaman. 'Your reaction in the penalty incident did you great honour. It is the kind of reaction which helps maintain the dignity of the game,' said FIFA general secretary Sepp Blatter, who knows all about the dignity of the game.

Fulham fans had a spell of enjoying waiting behind at the final whistle after a home win just to see John Pantsil go on a lap of honour. The full-back would run right round the pitch, waving to the crowd, blowing kisses, and clapping them for their support. And when Fulham beat Hamburg in the Europa League semi-final in 2010, he was so excited he lapped Craven Cottage twice. But Pantsil also sparked a diplomatic incident with his celebrations in Ghana's 2-0 win over the Czech Republic in the 2006 World Cup in Germany. Pantsil, who was playing club football for Israeli side Hapoel Tel Aviv at the time, pulled an Israel flag out of his sock after both goals and waved it at the cameras. A Ghana spokesman excused Pantsil by saying he was naïve and merely wanted to thank his fans in Israel for their support.

And finally in this chapter of controversies and confrontations, there was universal support and respect for young England international Jadon Sancho when he celebrated a hat-trick in the Bundesliga in May 2020. He took off his Borussia Dortmund top to reveal a yellow T-shirt calling for justice for George Floyd, whose horrific death a few turbulent days earlier had sparked worldwide protests. Sancho tweeted: 'My first professional hat-trick but a bitter sweet moment as there are more important things going on in the world. We have to come together and fight for justice.'

8

Passion: Unloading emotional baggage

LET IT all out, Stuart, don't hold anything back. His successful penalty in a tense shoot-out for England against Spain in Euro 96 was greeted by Stuart Pearce with a mixture of anger, relief, delight (OK, he didn't show that one) and venom. He blasted the ball home and advanced towards the crowd, punching the air vigorously and shouting. 'Come on' were probably the most printable words among his invective.

What had so wound him up? Well his pen was crucial as it helped England to a 4-2 shoot-out success and a place in the semi-final. Where, of course, they were knocked out by Germany, almost inevitably, in a penalty shoot-out after a 1-1 draw. No, what Pearce was remembering – as were all the Wembley crowd that day – was a previous penalty shoot-out involving England and Germany in a major tournament. That was the World Cup in 1990 when misses from the spot by Pearce and Chris Waddle gave West Germany the victory. Pearce's penalty that day was straight and true, but too straight as it hit the diving keeper's legs and bounced out. Pearce has never been one to hide his emotions and to say that his face rather gave away the fact that he was disappointed is a bit of an understatement. His team-mates consoled him but, bitterly upset, he left the field in tears. So 1996 and the goal against Spain somewhat atoned for it, and Pearce kept up his determined and single-minded approach to penalty-taking by being one of the successful kickers in what turned out to be the 6-5 defeat by Germany on penalties for a place in the final.

Pearce, or Psycho as fans called him, spent a whole career as one of the most committed of footballers, but he clearly had a few doubts when he was starting out. He made a late entry into the full-time game after training as an electrician, and even advertised his work as a sparky in the Nottingham Forest programme when he joined them. If Pearce was keen to earn a bit of money from outside football, then he got his chance with a famous Pizza Hut advert, joining Chris Waddle and Gareth Southgate in poking fun at themselves over missing crucial penalties in international showdowns. Pearce went on to have a long and successful career in the game and when he played for England at the age of 37 he became the third-oldest outfield player ever to appear for the country, behind Stanley Matthews and

Leslie Compton. And we all know where Southgate ended up.

Joy? Pride? Excitement? Stuart Pearce showed all of those, mixed with a dose of anger. Temur Ketsbaia was an angry man, too, when he scored a last-minute winner for Newcastle against Bolton at St James' Park in January 1998. So furious that his goal celebration is still remembered by the Geordie faithful as probably the most iconic they've ever seen.

The Newcastle striker had been seriously annoyed at being dropped to substitute and was raging when he came off the bench late in the game. So when he rammed the ball in at the far post, the emotions were still running incredibly high. He whipped off his shirt, tried to do the same with his boots, shrugged off a concerned team-mate and began viciously kicking the advertising hoardings. Lucky, on reflection, that he didn't get his boots off …

The fans loved it – his passion matched their inevitably high expectations of a Newcastle player – but Ketsbaia, once he'd calmed down, regretted it. 'I did much better things in Newcastle, and people only remember this one!' the Georgian international said in an interview with the Newcastle *Chronicle* much later. 'It was a bad moment for me, I just lost my control. Nobody's let me forget it. It wasn't a normal celebration, but I play with passion and all I wanted to do was play. It was not malicious.' And after becoming a coach when his playing days were over, he conceded: 'I understand this is not the way that a player should behave. I wouldn't be happy as their coach, but then I would admire the passion.' He can make as many excuses as he likes for his behaviour, but Newcastle fans won't ever forget Ketsbaia and his moment of madness. Players continue to kick the hoardings there – Aleksandar Mitrovic was one after scoring a penalty against Manchester United in 2016. But no one's ever done it with quite as much conviction and fury as Temur.

While Ketsbaia's non-celebrating celebration was born out of anger, Son Heung-Min's non-celebrating celebration came from compassion. The South Korean international scored twice for Spurs in their Champions League 4-0 win at Red Star Belgrade on 6 November 2019. His intention was obvious after his first goal. He found the nearest TV camera, solemnly bowed his head, and clasped his palms together in apology. Son was very keen to be seen to say sorry for his unintentional part in what looked an horrific ankle injury suffered by Everton midfielder Andre Gomes in a Premier League match just three days earlier. A distressed Son was sent off for his tackle on Gomes, though the red card was later rescinded. And Gomes himself was back playing after three months out. 'I'm really sorry for the accident and it's been a really tough few days,' Son said afterwards. 'I am lucky with all the support I have had from the fans and my team-mates.'

Charlie George's famous FA Cup Final goal celebration was also born from a flash of anger – or at least the feeling of being a bit pissed off, as he would put it. He celebrated one of Arsenal's best ever moments, his Wembley winner against Liverpool in extra time to complete the 1971 double, by lying flat-out on his back with his arms outstretched and a big grin on his face.

The story started when Arsenal beat Manchester City on a wet Maine Road night in the fifth round on their way to the final. George said much later, as reported in the *Daily Mail*, that his team-mate Frank McLintock pulled him out of the dressing room before the game and said he'd just been talking to City's assistant manager Malcolm Allison and he thought George was useless. Charlie said: 'I'd already scored one when I picked the ball up on the halfway line, they keep backing off and I keep going and smack it in the corner. 2-0 up, so I run back and lay down on my back, looking at Malcolm Allison. After the game I'm chasing him up the tunnel, swearing and calling him every name under the sun. He hasn't got a clue what's going on. But Frank made it all up. He went to see Malcolm and apologised.' What a wind-up. What a hugely successful wind-up.

The escapade that earned Craig Bellamy the nickname 'The Nutter with the Putter' could have blighted his reputation forever. So what did Bellamy do? He incorporated it into his next goal celebration, that's what. The volatile Bellamy has had his fair share of scrapes during a career of ups and downs, but the most notorious was on a Liverpool training trip to Portugal in 2007. A night out ended with Bellamy apparently losing his temper with team-mate John Arne Riise and lashing out at his legs with a golf club. In the cold light of day, both players apologised and accepted fines of two weeks' wages. Spat over, done and dusted, put to bed.

Until the next match, a Champions League game with mighty Barcelona. On scoring the equaliser for Liverpool, Bellamy celebrated by swinging an imaginary golf club. If anybody thought the celebration was in bad taste, Bellamy had the last word by setting up Liverpool's second goal for, of all people, Riise. As Liverpool manager Rafa Benitez said with prescience after the Portugese incident: 'Those kind of things don't make any difference on the pitch.'

Another Liverpool striker who liked to play a golf stroke after scoring was Emile Heskey. His trademark celebration, though, followed a trip to nightspot Ayia Napa in the summer of 2000 with a group of friends. When he scored he became a DJ, clamping one hand to an imaginary headphone on his ear with the other spinning a record. He also liked his golf shot, and he managed to squeeze in both celebrations, albeit briefly, after scoring in probably the most memorable game of his career. That was in Munich in 2001 when he got the final goal in England's 5-1 win in a World Cup qualifier against Germany.

Towards the end of a long and successful career, Heskey had a spell in Australia, playing for Newcastle

Jets, and the fans were certainly 'lovin' it' when he scored for them. Everyone in the crowd had been promised a free McDonald's milkshake if he found the net, and Heskey duly obliged. 'They were a happy crowd,' he confirmed afterwards. Milkshakes all round.

It cost him a booking but it was sweet revenge for Ruud van Nistelrooy when he scored for the Netherlands in a World Cup qualifier against Andorra on 7 September 2005. A prolific goalscorer for his country and for Manchester United during a 150-goal stay at Old Trafford, van Nistelrooy slipped up when he hit the post with a penalty in the match with Andorra. One of the opposition defenders made a point of mocking him by provocatively grinning into his face. It didn't take long for van Nistelrooy to have the last laugh. He scored at the far post – Netherlands won the match 4-0 – and looked round for his irritating opponent. He ran across, stood right in front of the man who had laughed at him, and raised his arms high in the air in celebration. Van Nistelrooy was yellow-carded for his unsportsmanlike behaviour. And it wasn't the first time van Nistelrooy had been provoked by opponents – a fiery Manchester United match with Arsenal at Old Trafford which ended goalless a couple of years earlier finished with opponents pushing and abusing him. By coincidence, he'd hit the woodwork with a penalty in that match too.

Robin van Persie emulated van Nistelrooy by playing for both the Netherlands and Manchester

United, and he also took off one of his goal celebrations to land himself in hot water. Playing for Fenerbahce in 2017, van Persie got the only goal of a Turkish Cup tie against Besiktas. He then slid on his knees to provocatively celebrate right in front of opposition player Oguzhan Ozyakup, who he'd clashed with earlier in the game. Funnily enough, they're fellow countrymen and, even weirder, they were mates when they were together at Arsenal earlier in their careers. Van Persie picked up a three-match ban for his behaviour.

This is the way it goes: attack builds up. Anticipation soars. Player scores. Decides where to celebrate. Runs there. Celebrates with something pre-planned or off the cuff. Trots back to own half, milking it by acknowledging the crowd, the bench, the missus … But not if you're England international Ross Barkley. He turned it all upside down when he scored Everton's final goal in a 6-3 win over Bournemouth in the Premier League on 4 February 2017. He celebrated. And then he scored.

It was well into injury time when Barkley ran on to a pass from Ramiro Funes Mori and went round Bournemouth goalkeeper Artur Boruc to leave himself with an open goal. Certain he was about to score – well, we all could have done from that position – Barkley raised both arms to the joyous Goodison faithful before rolling the ball into an empty net.

This goal's for you. Lots of players acknowledge their own team's supporters with their celebration but

Zimbabwe striker Benjani Mwaruwari had a special way of doing it. When he scored, he ran to the fans and pointed at them three times. He explained: 'I'm addressing myself to the fans and saying "I like you. And you. And you."' Awww …

Benjani's best time during his career in England was at Portsmouth, but although he was far from successful in his two-year stay at Manchester City, starting in 2008, he was loved by the fans. And he endeared himself to them even more when he made a cameo appearance during Vincent Kompany's testimonial game at City in 2019. Even at the grand old age of 41, he rose highest to head a goal past Shay Given two minutes from the end – and there was enough time, thank goodness, to give his 'I like you' pointy celebration one more outing.

Getting fined £1,500 for improper conduct was tough for Hermann Hreidarsson after he went a bit mad celebrating a goal he hadn't even scored. When Ipswich netted against Bradford in 2001 he dived head first into the crowd in delight, not realising colleague Mark Burchill had actually got the crucial final touch. Iceland international Hreidarsson apologised for what was literally an over-the-top celebration and said he was just so excited at thinking he'd scored his first goal at Portman Road.

As he was uncapped, unemployed, and hadn't played for months, when Brazil gave Josimar a shock late call to join their 1986 World Cup squad, it was no surprise that he didn't have a celebration planned in the unlikely event that he scored. After all, he was a full-back, so he needed to find one quickly when he scored past Northern Ireland keeper Pat Jennings in a group match with a shot that fizzed into the far corner from fully 30 yards. So Josimar simply legged it. Both arms fully raised, head back, he just sprinted wherever he felt like going, his face a picture of delight and, possibly, even a bit of shock. His fairy-tale World Cup ended with him being included in the team of the tournament and voted the most beautiful player, too. Good on you, Josi.

How not to get a good write-up for your performance. Samir Nasri scored for France against England in Euro 2012 and then ran towards French journalists in the press box with his finger on his lips. It was a none-too-subtle silencing gesture aimed at sports writers for previous criticisms. He quit international football a couple of years later at the young age of 27.

If he'd behaved himself he would have been good enough to play for England. But Robin Friday never could behave himself, on or off the field, and sadly died of a heart attack at the age of 38. A book about his extraordinary and short life, *The Greatest Footballer You Never Saw*, was published posthumously.

He served time in borstal and prison, took drugs and smoked, drank to excess, but was still voted Cardiff City's all-time top cult hero – even though he only played 20 games for them! And even though he'd been arrested when he turned up to sign for them after travelling by train from Reading with just a platform ticket.

His celebrations, both at Cardiff and Reading, the only two pro clubs he played for, were just as legendary. After scoring a last-minute winner for Reading against Rochdale he celebrated by running behind the goal and kissing a policeman. (Who remembers when police officers were on duty at football matches?) He said he felt sorry for the officer as he looked a bit cold and fed up so he decided to cheer him up, but is said to have told his team-mates he wished he hadn't done it as he hated the police. An even more memorable celebration took place on 16 April 1977 when Cardiff were playing Luton. He'd clashed several times with Luton goalkeeper Milija Aleksic so when he scored against him, Friday jogged past the keeper and gave him a V-sign. The picture of that two-fingered salute was later used on the front cover of a single by Cardiff group Super Furry Animals called 'The Man Don't Give A Fuck'. Says it all, really.

9

Team game:
A load of ducks

THE POINT of a celebration is to enhance the joy of a goal. But the young footballers of Icelandic team FC Stjarnan do it the other way round. For them, the point of a goal is to spark off an elaborate pre-rehearsed, heavily choreographed celebration. They must spend almost as much time on the training ground working out what to do when they score, as planning how they're actually going to get a goal in the first place. They've done everything from dancing to rowing, shooting, using a toilet, going on a bobsleigh and riding a bike.

The Stjarnan players reckon celebrations in other countries are dull and repetitive and they've advanced the golden moments of games into an art form. Catch their angling routine if you get the chance; it's one of their funniest ever. The goalscorer pretends to be fishing and a player mimics the fish caught on the line, writhing and wriggling along the ground as the angler reels him in. Half-a-dozen players then pick up the 'fish', tilt him lengthways in their arms, and pose for the 'photographer' (yes, another player) to get the picture of their 'big one'. It sounds a bit complicated written down, but it's LOL if you look it up on YouTube.

To enjoy such a choreographed routine by a whole team in England you probably have to go back more than 20 years and drop out of the Football League altogether. Aylesbury United are a relatively little non-league team who might have stayed in comparative obscurity for ever. But their clever and unique celebration was captured by TV cameras so it could be repeated time and time again. And its longevity was assured by the long-running TV quiz show *They Think It's All Over*. The players of Aylesbury got their 15 minutes of fame when they were invited to repeat their celebration in the 'Feel the Sportsman' round. That's when the contestants are blindfolded and have to guess what's going on in front of them.

What happened was that whenever Aylesbury scored during an epic FA Cup run in 1994/95, the players all got down on their knees and pretended to be ducks as they waddled in single file towards the dug-out. The club's nickname is The Ducks, after Aylesbury Ducks, which were first bred in the Buckinghamshire town in the 18th century. Aylesbury reached the first round proper of the FA Cup and introduced the duck walk when they beat fellow non-league side Newport IOW 3-2. There was no stopping them and it carried on in the next round when they won 4-1 at Kingstonian. The FA Cup dream came to a crashing end in the third round at QPR as they went down 4-0. No chance of their by-now famous goal celebration then? Well, no way were they going to duck out of a final chance to show it off and Aylesbury's players repeated it for their fans after the game anyway.

Also in the 1990s and also in the FA Cup, Watford got a lovely goal against Wimbledon and brought out a preconceived celebration known as the dead ants. It involved half-a-dozen players lying on their backs and kicking their legs furiously in the air. Not that dead ants do much kicking. What made it so much more memorable was Wimbledon's Mick Harford taking exception to their fun and marching straight through the huddle on the ground with not a glance at where he was planting his feet.

It's a great idea for supporters to have their own unique celebration but there's a flaw in the Poznan celebration as it involves turning your back on the pitch. So what's the point of that? Fans of the Polish club Lech Poznan started it way back in time, turning their backs on the game, joining arms and jumping up and down together when they had something to cheer about. They did it when their team played Manchester City in the Europa League on 21 October 2010 and the impressed City fans subsequently adopted it for themselves. But once rival fans began to jeeringly copy it if they managed to score a goal against City, then the celebration was dropped like the proverbial hot potato.

Cardiff City fans' signature celebration since 1990 has been doing the Ayatollah. It involves putting both hands above the head and moving them up and down in a patting motion. It was originally performed by the singers and followers of U Thant, a Welsh-language punk group, and adopted by football fans soon after. Former Cardiff players have taken it with them to other clubs and have been known to perform it – especially if they score down the road at Swansea.

Football supporters from Japan and Senegal had high praise heaped on them when they abandoned post-match celebrations of victories in the 2018 World Cup to clean the stadium around them. Japan beat Colombia 2-1 in Saransk, Russia, in their opening group game and turned their back on the pitch afterwards, getting bin bags out to make sure everything in the ground was left spick and span. Senegal fans followed the example and after their team won 2-1 against Poland in their opening match they cleaned all the litter away from their section of the Spartak Stadium in Moscow.

It was shocking but it was also reckoned to be the best on-field goal celebration at the 2018 World Cup. Yerry Mina got the only goal of the game as Colombia beat Senegal 1-0 to advance through the group stage. The Colombian players stood together in line and joined hands, and after Davinson Sanchez started it with a body pop all the players pretended an electric shock had gone through them one by one. It ended at the other end of the line with Mina, who went on to share the record for most goals scored by a defender in the World Cup finals. He got his third in the tournament when he scored against England in the next round before Colombia went out in a penalty shoot-out.

A couple of tournaments earlier, the 2010 World Cup had got off to a special start with hosts South Africa scoring the first goal of the tournament and celebrating it in style. It was the first time an African nation had hosted the World Cup and the atmosphere was special as Siphiwe Tshabalala found the net with a screamer in the opening game against Mexico in what commentator Peter Drury called 'a goal for all of Africa'. Half the delighted South African team raced to the touchline for a lovely little co-ordinated dance which some called a Macarena and others a Diski Dance. The Macarena originated in Spain while the Diski is a slang word for football in South African townships – in truth, the players' dance probably mixed moves from both of them. Though it started so stunningly for them, South Africa went out of the tournament after the group stage.

It might have been 'fair play' but it was a celebration that went wrong. The Romania team at the 1998 World Cup agreed that if they qualified from their group with a game to spare, they would all dye their hair blond. Well they did just that, and reluctant as some of them were, in came the hairdressers and transformed their crowning glories. It was meant to inspire team spirit but one of them complained of being left with a burnt scalp and bald patches and Romania failed to win their next two matches and crashed out of the tournament. It's a lovely thought that journalists covering the games could no longer distinguish the players from each other because, with their matching short blond hair, they all looked the same! Wonder why no other team has tried to repeat that particular celebration?

Back to celebrating with their own fans, and that's what the players of Swedish league side Gefle IF did after an away win over Kalmar in October 2016. Well *the* fan anyway. There's a touching picture of the players with their arms high in the air at the end of the match to acknowledge the one supporter who had made the 700-mile midweek round trip to watch his team. The fan, wearing gloves and hat on a chilly evening, looks suitably delighted with the special attention his heroes are all giving him. If not a little embarrassed too …

While that fan had superstar status, the same couldn't be said for a Southampton supporter at their League Cup tie with local rivals Portsmouth in September 2019. While all the fans around him celebrated a Saints goal in a 4-0 win, he was caught on camera with his head down searching in his pocket for his phone. When he found it, he then filmed himself celebrating, while everyone else had finished.

Social media subsequently dug him out mercilessly for his actions.

It was a great and good-humoured effort by Wolves fans to set up fake celebrations in a bid to wind up Liverpool supporters at Anfield. Liverpool needed Manchester City to lose to Brighton on the final day of the 2018/19 season to grab the title from them. So when the rumour started by Wolves fans spread around the ground that City were losing, they were undoubtedly delighted. In actual fact, Brighton scored soon after that anyway, but City were level within 83 seconds and went on to win the match and the title. What spoils this story, of course, is that Liverpool fans in this age of technology would have been all over the score at City, and would have realised they were being wound up. It's hard, though, to disagree with the fan who tweeted: 'Wolves fans pretending Brighton have scored at Anfield ... this is the type of shithousery I approve of.'

England fans who switched off the TV in abject disappointment as soon as their team were humiliated by Iceland in Euro 2016 missed a 'goosebumps' moment – though there was more than enough news coverage and action replays to catch up with it later. The Iceland players copied a unique celebration their fans had unveiled during the tournament – a sort of footballing version of New Zealand rugby's haka. It starts with hands raised high for a slow handclap, interspersed with a chant of an elongated 'huh', and builds with speed and noise to everyone clapping madly together at the end. It relies entirely on teamwork, and that, of course, was the secret of the players' success on the field. It looks and sounds for all the world like a Viking ritual, going back to the days of Icelandic marauding and pillaging (though, admittedly, no video coverage survives from 1,000-plus years ago). But realistically the 'huh' – or 'thunderclap' as it's often called – goes all the way back to 2014 and a match in Scotland. It was between Motherwell and Icelandic side Stjarnan (celebrities already in this chapter) when the teams met in the qualifying rounds of the Europa League. So impressed were the Iceland players with the home fans' innovative celebration that they reported back about the emotion stirred up by it. And the idea took hold.

The thunderclap was adopted by the Iceland supporters, and it was reckoned as many as one-tenth of the country's 330,000 population followed the team to France in 2016 for their first ever major tournament. But it wasn't just the chant that enchanted – England were terrible that night in Nice but Iceland's players and their fans thoroughly deserved the win and the glory. At the end, captain Aron Gunnarsson – who, with his full beard, looks exactly like the Viking warriors we remember pictured in school books on the subject – stood the players in formation in front of the fans and they all 'huh-ed' together. Slowly does it at first, then gathering noise and momentum to a gloriously joyous climax. Happy days.

10

Family affairs: One for you, Gran

WE'D ALL love to celebrate a goal with our 82-year-old grandmother, but it's not always possible. Unless your name's Alessandro Florenzi, as that's just what the Italian international did after scoring for Roma against Cagliari in 2014. He ignored his team-mates, raced off the pitch by the dug-outs, vaulted a barrier and ran up the steps into the main stand at the Olympic Stadium. And there was gran, watching young Alessandro play a match for the first time in her long life.

They hugged jubilantly before the Roma midfielder trotted back to the pitch to be met by an unsympathetic referee brandishing a yellow card. Perhaps the ref's own grandma couldn't make it that day. Alessandro said afterwards his grandmother had said she would come to her first ever match as long as he made time to say hello to her. But it cost him.

He broke the club's code of conduct for picking up an unnecessary booking and was fined for his gesture, though Roma coach Rudi Garcia commented: 'He will be happy to pay it. It was a beautiful image, to see his grandmother so delighted and moved. I love to see moments like this.'

The goal against Cagliari was by no means Florenzi's best in a Roma shirt. That came in September 2015 against Barcelona in a 1-1 draw in the European Champions League. Just over the halfway line, and right out by the touchline, he hit an extraordinary 60-yard Beckham-style wonder goal over the keeper into the far corner. His celebration that time was more muted. He put his hands over his eyes as if he was about to burst into tears before being pounced on by his mates. 'I honestly didn't know how to celebrate it,' he admitted.

Another 'goalscorer' who sneaked off for a celebratory kiss was the Brazilian player Wanderson after heading one in for Ludogorets late in a Bulgarian league match in August 2019 against Slavia Sofia. He ran off the pitch and waited for his wife to trot down to the front of the grandstand to give him a smacker on the lips for being such a clever boy. Unfortunately for Wanderson, the goal had been disallowed for offside – wrongly, as it turned out! – and the match had restarted without him, going on to end 0-0. His face as he turned back to the game was a picture. If a Hollywood actor had been asked to portray amazement and disappointment turning to fury in one look, he couldn't have done it more convincingly.

Now, if it had been Roy Keane who'd scored for Manchester United, I wonder what the reaction would have been if Gary Neville decided to kiss him in celebration? Mind you, Paul Scholes was pretty tough, too, and he didn't look exactly thrilled about it. Neville landed his smacker – right on the lips, too – after Scholes had headed a dramatic late winning goal against Manchester City in 2010. The pair had hugged in celebration before Neville moved in, cupping Scholes' head with both hands before the brief kiss. After his retirement Neville explained to an audience at the Oxford Union: 'Against City and Liverpool I couldn't control my emotions. If we scored a late winner I did stupid things, like kissing Scholesy.'

It's not unheard of for other footballers to have the occasional snog after scoring, but the most loving kiss was the one Laurent Blanc used to give French team-mate Fabien Barthez before 1998 World Cup matches. Even though Barthez was the team's goalkeeper, Blanc was the taller man and he used to have to bend slightly to give his mate a pre-match peck on his shiny bald pate. Not any old kiss, though, as Blanc would hesitate before lovingly picking out the exact spot for his smacker. The French public adored it, team-mates welcomed it as a great superstition, and everyone was mortified when Blanc was suspended for the final against Brazil. No problem, he emerged for the symbolic pre-match kiss anyway, and France went on to win the match and become world champions.

A kiss for a very different reason was how Grant Leadbitter celebrated his first goal for his local club Sunderland from 25 yards after coming on as a substitute against Arsenal on 4 October 2008. He raced to the team's technical area and knelt to kiss the grass nearby. It was where his dad Brian's ashes had been buried just a few weeks earlier.

There were all sorts of theories about what Kevin De Bruyne meant by his celebration when he scored for Manchester City against Spurs in December 2017. Normally a quiet celebrator of goals, and very quick to point at a team-mate in gratitude for an assist, this time he was quite animated as he held up two fingers on one hand and one on the other. 2-1? What does that mean? A reference to a previous win by that score over Manchester United? Or to the 21-point lead they held over a rival team in the Premier League? Well, no, it was signifying the number 21, as worn by fellow City star David Silva who was absent from the team that day. Silva, in fact, had just become the father of a very premature baby son and was away on compassionate leave. The baby, Mateo, spent five months in hospital but survived and Silva now has a tattoo on his arm in honour of the little boy, joining another tattoo on his wrist in memory of a five-year-old cousin who died of cancer. Honouring them is part of Silva's goal celebrations.

Another goal celebration dedicated to family has been the crossed arms, with fingers pointing, by Polish striker Robert Lewandowski. It's been seen many times as Lewandowski has proved an outstanding goalscorer in German football, but he will only say that it's to do with his daughter Klara, the actual explanation remaining his secret. What Lewandowski did say was: 'That moment when you score a goal and 80,000 fans cheer your name is a really special feeling. You get goosebumps and just want to fly.' Or cross your arms and point your fingers …

The second teenager ever to score in a World Cup Final – the one and only Pele was the first – Kylian Mbappe has a celebration all of his own. Well, his own apart from his kid brother Ethan who he stole it from. The young striker, whose goals helped France win the 2018 World Cup tournament, celebrated by crossing his arms with his thumbs pointing up while kneeling on the ground. His brother did it after winning a game of FIFA against him, and he decided to copy it.

Mbappe declined to do his trademark celebration when he scored for Paris Saint-Germain in January 2020 because it was against his old club AS Monaco. But when he got his second in a 4-1 win, he couldn't resist, obviously deciding he'd already paid his respects first time around. Just a couple of weeks earlier, Mbappe's crossed-arm celebration turned up in the Premier League when Liverpool's Trent Alexander-

Arnold raced to the club's fans after scoring in a 4-0 win at Leicester and stood in front of them in the pose. Far from being put out that his trademark was being copied, Mbappe generously told BBC Sport: 'Yeah, I saw! I'm proud, this guy is amazing.'

Not many two-year-olds get to have their suggestion for a goal celebration used in the Premier League, which makes Nia Barnes pretty special. Burnley striker Ashley Barnes introduced his unique goal celebration at the start of the 2019/20 season at the request of his daughter. It involved putting his hands horizontally across his face with two fingers from each hand masking his eyes; a bit like Dele Alli's hard-to-do hand gestures. Good old Ashley reckoned little Nia is better at doing the celebration than proud dad!

Sheffield United captain Billy Sharp was another who had family reasons for his celebration after he came on as a sub and scored to put his team through to the FA Cup quarter-finals with victory over Reading on 2 March 2020. He imitated a flapping bird, explaining to *Sheffield United News* afterwards: 'My oldest son at the moment is playing a lot of FIFA. He's pestering me to do the celebrations and asking "Dad, can you do this?" So, hopefully, he sees that tomorrow and it'll make him smile!'

Mateo Kovacic put his thumb on his nose and wiggled his fingers, in the way we used to do as kids if we were being daringly rude to someone, when he scored for Chelsea against Valencia in the Champions

League in November 2019. But he wasn't insulting anyone – it was a gesture beloved by his two nieces and was especially for them to enjoy.

Crossing his arms and looking grumpy was the way Republic of Ireland international Ronan Curtis chose to celebrate his goal for Portsmouth against Barnsley in the FA Cup fourth round in January 2020. And, of all people, the celebration was dedicated to his mum, Marie. He told the club website his mother told him she had a gut feeling he wouldn't score that day so when he proved her wrong it was dedicated to her. Bet they had a good conversation over breakfast the next morning.

Also with family in mind was Uruguayan Nicolas Lodeiro, who built up a reputation for taking his boot off after scoring and pretending to use it as a phone. When he first started playing, his dad couldn't get to all his games, so a phone call home became their tradition together.

Whose goal celebration has been the most repeated in football history? Step forward Bebeto, a key member of Brazil's team that won the World Cup in 1994. The celebrations happened in a much-awaited quarter-final against Holland, a game that turned out to be the best in the whole tournament, with Brazil winning 3-2. It was certainly loads better than a disappointing final when Brazil beat Italy on penalties. Anyway, Bebeto picked up the ball about 35 yards out from the Dutch goal, controlled it on his thigh, and raced past the covering defender. He rounded the keeper, popped the ball into the empty net, and the celebration began. Bebeto ran off towards the touchline, rocking an imaginary baby in his arms. Two mates, Romario and Mazinho, joined him on either side and the three of them stood there together, grinning and rocking. Bebeto had just become a dad for the third time and the celebration was in honour of his new baby. Bebeto explained: 'It was something from God, something from the heart, spontaneous. Because of this it went down in history.' These days that baby boy Mattheus Oliveira is himself a successful pro footballer and that rocking celebration is repeated all around the world wherever and whenever a player has just become a dad.

Another player with babies on the brain once did a goal celebration that was funny and unique, while another of his was much-copied and, well, nauseating. Francesco Totti had a great, World Cup-winning career, and was one of those annoying footballers who seemed to have everything. Good looks, a model wife, top goalscorer ever for his club Roma, and that World Cup glory with Italy in 2006.

It was his celebration of a goal for Roma in a derby match with Lazio in November 1998 that gained him worldwide attention. He lay on his back and stuffed the ball up his shirt to mimic being heavily pregnant. And then lay back while his team-mates removed the 'baby'. It was a tribute to his missus, who was expecting their child – bet she was made up with him for it.

Later in his career he adopted the thumb-suck, a yucky celebration that was much copied by others and it looked no better when anyone else did it than in the Totti original. It was thought to be a reference to his young children, but you can't keep his wife Ilary out of the picture. 'I have this defect, which I do with my thumb all the time, so Francesco does it for me,' she said.

So, in reality, it's one of three choices of celebration for a player who's just become a parent or is about to become one. Either the Bebeto baby-rocking movement, a good old thumb-suck, or the ball stuck up the shirt in a heavily-pregnant gesture. Dad-to-be Raul Jimenez went for the latter when he scored for Wolves in their 3-0 win over Norwich on 23 February 2020. It was just the goal to do it with, as he was less than a yard out and it meant he could thrash the ball over the line and immediately grab it from the back of the net to give himself a nine-month stomach bulge.

Going back to Italian footballers, they've always taken their celebrations pretty seriously and former international striker Vincenzo Montella knew exactly what he was going to do whenever he scored. Which was pretty often in his heyday. His celebration earned him a nickname – Aeroplanino – which stuck with him throughout his career. Montella, who had a spell at Fulham after years of goalscoring in Italy, spread his arms wide and swooped from side to side after a goal. Yes, like an aeroplane. Well, a little aeroplane to be exact, as *aeroplanino* means small plane and Montella himself is no giant.

A World Cup winner with Germany who also enjoyed club football success in England, Spain and the Bundesliga, Mesut Ozil has a misunderstood goal celebration. When he shaped his hand into a letter M after scoring, people took it as standing for his first name. But no, M is for his little niece, Mira, his brother's first child, who has brought much happiness to the family. 'I want to show her how much I love her so when I score a goal, I do this M,' he said.

If not for his long and successful career, Ozil deserves to be remembered for the generous gesture he and his bride Amine made for their June 2019 wedding. Instead of traditional gifts, they asked guests to donate to a charity which funds life-changing operations for children in developing countries who suffer from burns, club feet, and cleft lip and palate. As a footballer in a fortunate and privileged position, he said he and his wife would be funding surgery for 1,000 children in need. Good old M for Mesut.

England international Paul Ince celebrated with a somersault and an amusing sort of sideways full-length dive after one goal he scored while playing for Inter Milan and in more than 500 games at the top level in England he had plenty more opportunities to enthusiastically join in and lead goal celebrations. But nothing could quite match the sheer pleasure of his joyful celebration caught live by BT cameras in December 2017, when he was working as a pundit and his son Tom scored for Huddersfield. Proud dad doesn't quite do it justice.

It looked like a publicity stunt for Nike when Brazilian superstar Neymar balanced his new boot on his head after scoring for Paris Saint-Germain against Amiens in January 2018. Not so, said Neymar, even though Nike is one of his sponsors. He revealed on Instagram it was a birthday tribute to a friend back in Brazil. The following year a more restrained Neymar celebrated a goal for PSG by putting a finger on his lips and bowing his head to signify it was a time for quiet. He said: 'The idea is to forget everything else, to talk less and play more.'

The best known hand gesture celebrations by British sportsmen are not actually footballers, though. Cricket legend Ben Stokes celebrates by holding his right hand up with his middle finger half-furled. It's a tribute to his dad, Ged, who back in the day had part of his finger amputated so he could return more quickly to his career as a professional rugby league player. And talking of rugby, England rugby union captain Owen Farrell has a complicated-looking little gesture with both hands, twisting his figures into the initials JJ. It's in appreciation of youngster Jack Johnson, who suffers from muscle-wasting disease Duchenne muscular dystrophy. Farrell has done it for years and says the Joining Jack Campaign, which raises money for research into treatment for the disease, is a cause close to his heart. Ex-England and Manchester United defender Rio Ferdinand is one of many others who have also performed the 'Jack Salute'.

A forerunner for that gesture, also in a good cause, was taken up by several footballers a few years ago. Celebrating players, including Everton striker Andy Johnson, Manchester City defender Micah Richards and former Newcastle and Wigan defender Titus Bramble, were among those using their hands to form the letter A. It's done by pointing two fingers downwards with the index finger from the other hand forming the horizontal bar. The sign represented A-Star, a footballing initiative aimed at opening up pathways into employment for youngsters through sport and other creative activities. Fitz Hall, whose career took in Crystal Palace, Wigan, QPR and Watford, was a co-founder of the initiative and one of the first to unveil the A-sign. And his other claim to fame? The best ever footballing nickname: 'One-Size'.

They're not exactly family, but Pierre-Emerick Aubameyang and Alexandre Lacazette looked like brothers when they celebrated an Arsenal goal together against Newcastle in March 2019. Well, brothers born into a well-to-do family of 19th-century country gentlemen, at least. They respectfully shook hands as they bowed to each other. But not any old bow, it was a full-blown effort with heads dipped to about two feet above the ground and their left arms behind their backs in the most formal of manners. When you're friends off the pitch it's easier to play together on it, explained Lacazette of what looked for all the world like a bromance with his fellow striker.

Lacazette has form for bonding with team-mates and in 2017 he swopped celebrations with Corentin Tolisso, who he played with at French club Lyon. Instead of what was then his normal 'trumpet' celebration, Lacazette celebrated scoring for Arsenal by doing a Star Trek Vulcan salute, where two fingers point one way, and the other two point the other to form a V, leaving a gap in the middle. That was because his mate Tolisso normally uses the salute but the previous day had scored the winning goal for Bayern Munich against Hamburg and celebrated by bringing out the Lacazette 'trumpet' blow. That's nice, eh? Though there is a flaw in this story as Lacazette says his celebration is because his friend likes trumpet music, but it looks as though he's actually pretending to play a flute, not blowing his own trumpet.

11

Managers: Letting their hair down

WORLD CUP winners do it. So do teams who have just won the Champions League. But it seemed somewhat strange to see Liverpool do it after a 2-2 home draw with West Bromwich Albion in December 2015.

The celebration in question was for the whole team and manager – especially the manager in Liverpool's case – to stand in a row, link hands, and bow several times to the crowd. 'I wanted to say thank you to the supporters,' explained the then recently installed Liverpool manager Jurgen Klopp. 'You need moments like this that everybody can enjoy.' Klopp had previously had a bit of a pop at Liverpool fans for leaving early when the team were losing, and the gesture in front of the Kop was calculated to get them back onside. History tells us it worked a treat.

The excitable Klopp's always been a great celebrator of goals – whether it's high-fiving fans, pumping his fist, beating his chest, leaping into the air, running down the touchline or even on to the pitch, diving across the ground or kicking the hoardings. If there's a mob of players he'll happily join in too, jumping on top of them to help spread the love. It cost him a new set of spectacles when he leapt aboard the players' celebrations of Adam Lallana's injury-time winner at Norwich in 2016, Christian Benteke sending them flying in the melee. Klopp bought a new pair which he complained made him look like a serial killer after pointing out that he couldn't find his spare pair without having glasses for the search!

Building up a great rapport with the Anfield fans paid rich dividends at the end of that season, when Liverpool fought back from behind to beat Klopp's old team Borussia Dortmund in the Europa League quarter-finals. The unforgettable atmosphere created by the crowd played a huge part that night, captain Jordan Henderson acknowledging: 'The crowd kept with us. Even when we were getting beat, they kept us going. The fans were brilliant.'

Another time when Klopp's enthusiasm got the better of him was in December 2018 when Liverpool scored a late, late winner to beat Everton in the Merseyside derby. After Divock Origi netted deep into stoppage time, Klopp ran 60 yards on to the pitch and celebrated by hugging the slightly bemused Liverpool keeper Alisson. He was afterwards fined

£8,000 and accepted an FA misconduct charge, promising it wouldn't happen again and he would tone down his celebrations in future. It may not happen again, but it had happened before, while he was managing Mainz in Germany.

Klopp's involuntary celebration of Liverpool's derby winner had repercussions a few weeks later as Wolves manager Nuno Espirito Santo raced down the touchline to join in his players' celebrations after an injury-time winner in a 4-3 success against Leicester. The referee, Chris Kavanagh, was the same official who ignored it when Klopp ran on to the field at Anfield that day, and he'd clearly got in a bit of hot water for doing so, as this time he showed Nuno a red card for encroaching on the pitch. The manager said the emotion of the late winner got the better of him – 'I was sent off for it and it was the right decision,' he told BBC's *Match of the Day*.

Excitable and emotional as Klopp and Nuno proved to be, they're probably still more restrained than former Peterborough manager Barry Fry. When – or perhaps if – his team scored, he would set off on a mad, whooping, joyful, passionate run down the touchline. He'd high-five fans, shout his delight with the odd expletive thrown in, and trot back to the dug-out with a huge grin across his face. Of course, the supporters loved it and anticipated that joyous moment of celebration as much as the match itself.

Fry was a football boss for more than 30 years and was willing to expose his unique management style in a ground-breaking fly-on-the-wall TV documentary, *There's Only One Barry Fry*. Never has a reality show more accurately lived up to its name, as Fry's endearing enthusiasm for football and life spilled over. It's said that the first of his two heart attacks occurred when he was pushing the team bus at Peterborough, but it could easily have been made worse by those lung-busting touchline sprints ...

If we thought Fry had ended the run of managers sprinting up the line to celebrate goals, then Duncan Ferguson emotionally revived the tradition in Everton's 3-1 win over Chelsea on 7 December 2019. Ferguson, a former Scottish international striker with a tough-guy reputation, had only stepped up to the managerial hot seat in a caretaker capacity a couple of days earlier, after Marco Silva had been shown the door. But wearing his heart on his sleeve, he just couldn't help himself when Everton scored. He raced up the touchline – but what made it special was ball boys jumping into his arms as he did so. In a touching moment, he hugged and swung the delighted ball boys around before returning them to ground level. Not surprisingly, the crowd loved his instinctive outpouring of pure emotion. Ferguson said afterwards: 'When you see the kids' faces ... I think one of them was in tears and I was in tears to be honest.'

Those Everton ball boys weren't the only ones ever to get in on the act. Young Taylor Hunt couldn't stop himself when his team Wycombe Wanderers got a late equaliser against Dagenham & Redbridge in 2015. He forgot he was a ball boy and when he ran to join the celebrating players his day was made when Aaron Pierre lifted him out of the huddle and held him high in the air. The clip of the joyous moment went worldwide and Taylor soon found himself invited back to the club to give interviews far and wide about his moment as a celebrity.

Going back to managers, Graeme Souness admitted it wasn't the cleverest thing he's ever done, but he still had no regrets about planting his team's flag in the centre circle of their fiercest rival's pitch. The former Liverpool legend was celebrating a 1-1 draw for Galatasaray, the club he managed, in the final of the Turkish Cup on 24 April 1996. It gave them a 2-1 aggregate win over Fenerbahce and his flag gesture nearly sparked a riot in the home crowd.

Years later, Souness explained to Virgin Media Sport that a Fenerbahce director had questioned what Galatasaray were doing in choosing him, as he'd previously had open heart surgery. He said when it came to his turn to wave the giant flag he just thought he'd run to the halfway line and plant it to prove his fitness to the man who'd insulted him. Scotland international Souness called the time he spent in Turkey the most marvellous year of his football life.

Back when Blackpool had their one and only season in the Premier League – 2010/11 – their manager Ian Holloway had an interesting take on goal celebrations, when he said his players needed to celebrate goals for a bit longer. He said they were rushing back to restart the game and were still in a state of excitement and maybe not concentrating properly, while other clubs took up to two minutes celebrating goals and were calm and collected by the time the restart was taken. Food for thought.

If you're the second-choice goalkeeper, pushing over the manager in last-minute goal celebrations probably won't win you a precious place in the starting XI. Manchester City goalkeeper Ederson was so excited when Brazil scored against Costa Rica in a group match in the 2018 World Cup that he charged out of the substitutes' dug-out. Just ahead of him, manager Tite was also racing towards the pitch and when Ederson stumbled in the excitement of it all he pushed the boss in the back and sent him flying. The manager was quickly hauled back to his feet and the fun and games carried on …

Sometimes the story behind the celebration is better than the celebration itself. And sometimes it isn't. Lee Bradbury performed his set-piece routine to perfection after scoring for Bournemouth at Grimsby on 21 November 2008 in a 3-3 draw. As team-mates ran up in turn to congratulate him, Bradbury swung a fist at them, pretending to knock them out. A right, a left, a right … each player fell to the ground, seven of them in all. And what was his knockout celebration all about? Manager Jimmy Quinn had taken the Bournemouth squad for a boxing training session in a bid to toughen them up and Bradbury had obviously taken the lesson on board.

So famous was manager David Pleat's run across Manchester City's Maine Road pitch on the final afternoon of the 1982/83 season that the shoes he was wearing that day were later auctioned for £4,000. Pleat's much-watched celebratory jigging run came after his team Luton Town scored a late winner to avoid relegation and send City down instead. Much later, Pleat told the *Daily Mail*: 'I was like a crazy kangaroo, wasn't I? At the end I just instinctively ran on to the field. I have no idea what I was thinking about, it was the release of pent-up emotion. It was pride, that's what I felt.'

The crazy kangaroo wasn't the first manager to be remembered for celebrating on the pitch – Bob Stokoe, quite rightly, ran across Wembley to congratulate his hero goalkeeper Jim Montgomery after Second Division Sunderland had beaten then mighty Leeds in the 1973 FA Cup Final. Managers in the 21st century put a lot of stock by their appearance but what was so charming about Stokoe that day was not only the look of sheer delight on his face but also the clothes on his back. He wore a, frankly, slightly shabby-looking mac, red tracksuit trousers and topped off the ensemble with his trademark trilby hat. As a player he won an FA Cup winners' medal with Newcastle in 1955 and as a manager he had 12 jobs and was never sacked from any of them. Normally deadly rivals, Newcastle and Sunderland came together in mutual mourning when Stokoe sadly died in 2003.

It had been 26 years since Manchester United won the league, so no wonder manager Sir Alex Ferguson showed his joy when Steve Bruce headed home in the sixth minute of stoppage time to give his team a vital 2-1 victory over Sheffield Wednesday on 10 April 1993. Fergie raced out of his dug-out and did a little jump for joy as he celebrated the moment. Then something momentarily distracted him, and it was the sight of his assistant Brian Kidd racing past him and going down on his knees on the pitch to celebrate.

You've got to have some bravado to use a goal celebration to have a cheeky dig at your manager. Especially when the man in question is the very same and legendarily abrasive Sir Alex. Andy Cole had just scored a fine goal for Manchester United in a 3-3 draw at Barcelona in the Champions League in September 1998. He celebrated by running to an advertising board for Ford Focus and pointing at the word Focus. He told the *Manchester Evening News* long after he'd retired from playing: 'The manager told me off for messing about in training and was screaming that I needed to focus. I told the lads what I'd do if I scored.'

Alan Pardew resisted the urge to jump on the pitch when a late goal by Papiss Cisse gave the Newcastle team he was managing a 1-0 win over Fulham in April 2013. Instead, he jumped into the crowd. He emerged slightly dishevelled but none the worse for the experience, and explained it was just a spur of the moment decision caused by sheer delight at the winning goal.

12

Grounded: Taking the plunge and flagging it up

HOW DO you get from hate figure to folk hero in five seconds flat? To say that Jurgen Klinsmann wasn't particularly welcome when he signed for Spurs in 1994 is a bit of an understatement. Rightly or wrongly, he carried two very black marks by his name – he was German, and he had the reputation for being a diver. It's hard to know which of the two was thought to be worse, though of course the intolerance of Germans is a football one, simply because of so many penalty shoot-out disappointments.

Now picture the scene: it was Klinsmann's first game for Spurs, a 4-3 win at Sheffield Wednesday, and he scored the fourth with a header. Bring on one of the best ever goal celebrations. Klinsmann sprinted off and dived full length across the turf with his arms spread out, grinning self-mockingly from ear to ear. It was a clear reference to his reputation, and how we love someone who can laugh at themselves.

From that day, Klinsmann could do no wrong. He ended that season as Footballer of the Year and there was even a waxwork model of him in Madame Tussauds. His legendary status was enhanced by him driving around London in a VW Beetle, by his charity work, and his interest in the environment. That Jurgen, don't you just love him …

It's very easy to see from his face what was on the mind of Luis Suarez when he scored for Liverpool against Everton in a 2012 Merseyside derby. He brushed aside team-mates and ran to the halfway line before performing a comedy dive, throwing himself theatrically to the ground in front of the Everton dug-out. It was his response to some pre-match comments by Everton manager David Moyes about English football being ruined by players who dive. To his credit, Moyes took it in good part and said afterwards he quite liked the celebration. Suarez, who has scored goals for fun for Liverpool, Ajax and Barcelona, has a set routine when he finds the back of the net. First he kisses his ring finger as a dedication to his wife and long-time partner Sofia. Then he kisses two more fingers and a tattoo on his wrist of his daughter Delfina, all to show his love of his family. His celebration will last all his life as Suarez has immortalised it with a tattoo on his neck showing the exact positions of his fingers and wrist when he celebrates a goal.

This chapter is all about hitting the ground – and the most significant ever celebratory forward roll, followed immediately by a backflip, was performed by a delighted Michael Thomas after his legendary injury-time winning goal for Arsenal away to Liverpool on 26 May 1989. It was a championship decider in what in those days was Division One, with Arsenal needing to win by a two-goal margin to nick the title from Liverpool, who went into the match three points clear at the top. They got the first goal through Alan Smith and then Thomas dashed through the centre of the Liverpool defence in the last minute before coolly slotting past Bruce Grobbelaar to score the goal that gave Arsenal a 2-0 win and their first title for 18 years. Thomas's goal was voted the second greatest moment in Arsenal's history, while the player himself moved on to play for Liverpool, of all teams, a couple of years later.

Another one to end up flat on the ground, where he proceeded to crawl along on all fours after scoring for Nigeria in the 1994 World Cup, Finidi George then produced the amusing and even astonishing celebration of cocking his leg up in imitation of a urinating dog. The goal had been classy, chipping over out-rushing Greece keeper Adonis Minous; the celebration not so much. And no one's ever really got to the bottom of what it was all about.

Finidi – his name rather poetically means 'Future Full of Sun' in his native tongue – was at all other times a rather graceful player, who was outstanding in Europe for Ajax and Real Betis and even played in

England for Ipswich later in his career. His crowning glory was a Champions League medal when Dutch club Ajax won the 1995 final against AC Milan. Many years later, he rather coyly told an interviewer who asked about his amazing celebration: 'These are things of the past which I will not go into. If I said nothing at the time, I will not say anything now.' He may well have been taking the piss out of someone or something, but it looks like we're never going to find out for certain.

So what's the most dangerous don't-try-this-at-home-kids goal celebration? Step forward, or rather leap forward and fall flat on your stomach, Shefki Kuqi, a Kosovan Albanian who became a naturalised Finn and played for a number of Football League clubs in a long career. When he scored, he would run forward, jump into the air, and fall full length on the ground. His belly-flop celebration looked painful and dangerous, and in any case who wants to end up flat on their face munching grass when there's a goal to enjoy with your team-mates and fans? But it was all perfectly safe, Kuqi told the *East Anglian Daily Times*, so that's all right then. 'It is not dangerous at all,' he said, during his days with Ipswich. 'I perfected it in the swimming pool. People think I'm coming down on my chest but I'm not really, I come down on my hands to soften the impact, if I did come down on my chest it would hurt.' Yes, too right.

Shefki aside, the celebration by Portugal international Nani also looked unnervingly dangerous, and there was even talk of manager Sir Alex Ferguson banning it at Manchester United. Nani brushed colleagues away after scoring so that he could find a nice bit of empty pitch to work with. He then launched himself into a look-no-hands backflip, sometimes two of them and sometimes with a bit of a diver's twist as well. No wonder Sir Alex wasn't keen.

Nani – whose proper name is Luís Carlos Almeida da Cunha – had plenty of chances to show off his moves. There was a lovely moment on 30 July 2011, when he was playing for Manchester United in the pre-season Herbalife World Football Challenge and scored against Barcelona in a 2-1 win. Colleague Danny Welbeck ran respectfully alongside him and then did a little subconscious skip in time with Nani's spectacular gymnastics.

His celebration was not a random move because he was good at gym at school, but there was a childhood link. It's based on the *capoeira*, a Brazilian martial art that combines dance, acrobatics and music. The move is known as the mortal, or 'leap of death', which might have been thought of as a bit melodramatic, until an unfortunate Indian league footballer did actually die after damaging his spinal cord while attempting a backflip goal celebration.

Better than a Cruyff turn, better than a nutmeg, my own favourite football trick has always been when a player tucks a ball behind a defender on one side and runs past him on the other to continue bearing down on goal. Robbie Keane completed just such a manoeuvre before firing into the far corner on his way to a second-half hat-trick for Spurs against Everton on 12 January 2003. He followed up with his trademark celebration. He waved colleagues away, pointed his fingers while blowing a kiss, performed a cartwheel at full speed followed by a forward roll, finishing off with a double-handed pistol-shooting gesture as his mates moved in to mob him.

During an illustrious career, which included captaining the Republic of Ireland and playing club football on three different continents, Keane had lots of other celebrations as well. But the athletic, energetic and possibly dangerous cartwheel remained the one he was best known for. His own thoughts on why he did it were a bit vague, though: 'It didn't really come from anywhere, it's just something I made up myself,' he said once.

One thing's for certain – fans who arrived at a test event at Spurs' new stadium on 30 March 2019, when Inter Milan provided the opposition, were hoping for two things. One – that Keane would score; two – that when he did, he'd bring the cartwheel celebration out one more time. And they got their way. At the grand old age of 38, Keane didn't disappoint and after scoring in a nine-goal thriller he wheeled out his trademark move. Time stood still at that moment.

Forward rolls? Easy peasy. We learnt how to do them at primary school. But not somersaults five foot up in the air. Prolific goalscorer Robert Earnshaw was loved by the fans in a long career because the joy of scoring goals always just overwhelmed him. The somersault was his favourite, but at various other times he grabbed a TV mic to imitate a singer, stripped down to his waist, and pretended to be a matador. And a gold-digger. And a juggler. Though not all at once.

Familiar ground, this, but his trademark mid-air somersault wasn't so popular with his managers – Alan Cork fined him every time he flipping did one for Cardiff City. Earnie, as he was known, was born in Zambia where his dad managed a gold mine and his mum was a professional footballer before becoming a boxer. But he grew up in Wales and chose that as the country he'd represent. He played predominantly for Cardiff, starting in 1998 and ending in 2013 after spells in between at other clubs. His proud record is he's the only player to have scored hat-tricks in the Premier League, all three Football League divisions, the FA Cup, the League Cup and in international football. That's a record which is going to take some beating.

What Earnshaw has never achieved – as far as is known! – is the seven successive backflips Julius Aghahowa completed after he scored for Nigeria against Sweden in the 2002 World Cup. It gave them the lead in the match but they eventually went down 2-1. A pretty good goal it was, too, Aghahowa racing in to head home a cross from the right. One contemporary report said that his acrobatics took him from the goal area all the way to the halfway line in celebration. They didn't and it would have meant each backflip covering about eight yards at a time – he's good, but not that good. Sadly, Wigan fans never got to see his extravagant celebration. Aghahowa played 20 games for them in the Premier League but always stayed upright as he never found the net.

Perhaps they ask for a CV stating a striker must be able to do backflips, double somersaults and all manner of athletic celebrations if they sign for the club. Certainly, Newcastle United have had more than their fair share of goalscorers going head over heels in an extended period.

Faustino Asprilla was a high-profile member of the Newcastle squad in the 1995/96 season when manager Kevin Keegan blurted out that he'd love if it they could beat Manchester United to the title. They didn't, they finished second. Asprilla, a Colombian international who'd arrived to sign for Newcastle in February 1996 wearing a fur coat in a snowstorm, was loved for his athletic ahead-of-the-times somersault celebrations. He also picked up a booking for removing his shirt and swinging it from the corner flag after scoring against Metz in the UEFA Cup, meaning he was suspended from the next game.

Lomana LuaLua followed him a few years later and he was another who loved an acrobatic celebration. The striker, from DR Congo, also caused quite a stir when he scored for Portsmouth against Newcastle while on loan to them in 2004. He didn't hold back with the celebration of his 89th-minute equaliser, pointing out his name on the back of his

Portsmouth shirt to the Newcastle fans. In a deviation from a standard loan agreement, Newcastle had failed to include a clause banning their loaned-out player from playing against them, forcing a change in the laws forbidding on-loan players from playing against their parent club.

His ability to score goals saw Obafemi Martins take his football career all over the world – Italy, Germany, Russia, USA, China – not to mention Newcastle and a brief loan spell at Birmingham. And wherever he went, he took his spectacular goal celebration with him. The man whose first name means 'the king loves me', had an acrobatic backflip celebration where he got higher in the air than some players do for their headers.

Following in all their illustrious footsteps was Allan Saint-Maximin, who tumbled over at the double – forwards and then backwards – after scoring the winning goal for Newcastle at Southampton in March 2020. Though it hardly seemed possible, he endeared himself even more to the fans who had made the long journey south to support the team by giving his shirt away at the end to a young lad who had copied his appearance by wearing a dreadlocked wig and a bandana.

When the 'Digital Crawl' was invented, fans and team-mates loved it. But sharp-shooting Vitalis Takawira found himself in hot water with officials. And all because of TV. A Zimbabwean international, Vitalis was playing Major League Soccer in the US for Kansas City Wizards in the 1990s when he unveiled his way of marking a goal. He dropped on all fours and crawled along the pitch, team-mates either joining in behind, or lifting his legs to propel him along as if he was in a one-man wheelbarrow race. Vitalis, whose nickname is Digital, based his crawl celebration on Finidi George's infamous 'dog staking his territory' impression at the previous World Cup.

Referees in the States, though, were told to clamp down on it, fearing over-long celebrations would overrun the allocated two-hour time-slots for football matches on TV. Mind you, it was the inaugural year for Major League Soccer in the US, so perhaps undue deference was being shown to the broadcasting paymasters ... 'Digital' hit back at the time: 'I don't know why they stopped me. You must have your own style of celebrating. To me, that was the greatest thing to do, score a goal, and when you score, why wouldn't you want to celebrate? I just enjoy seeing players celebrate after a goal, because the bottom line is that we play to score goals.' Kansas City coach Ron Newman agreed. 'The referee was so busy trying to stop the crawl, but why? The fans love it. And anything to get the fans excited – that gets them talking – is good.'

Takiwara had a memorable international debut for Zimbabwe as the opponents were South Africa in their very first game after the ban because of apartheid was lifted. 'It was truly amazing,' he remembered: 'I honestly didn't think I was even going to play but the coach started me and I had a great game.' And why was he nicknamed Digital – or Didge, as his team-mates abbreviated it? 'I'm not sure, but I got it in Zimbabwe. When you graduate to a club's first team the supporters give you a nickname. Perhaps they thought I was quick and controlled, like something digital.' Yes, perhaps they did …

Talking of crawling, there's a young ball boy somewhere in Saudi Arabia who won't ever forget the time he encountered a trademark celebration by Bafétimbi Gomis. The French international striker's time at Swansea will be stored in Welsh memories, as after scoring he used to crawl on all fours, pretending to be a panther. After leaving Swansea, Gomis played for Marseille and Galatasaray before moving on to Saudi Arabia's Al-Hilal. When he scored his fifth goal in four games for the club, out came the usual crawl and he panther-prowled in the direction of a young ball boy. The youngster, quite understandably, took fright and decided on the sensible option of running in the opposite direction. The story has a happy ending as Gomis found the lad afterwards and gave him his No. 18 shirt.

How old do you have to be to give up doing your trademark goal celebration? Well, 34 – or that is certainly how old Miroslav Klose was when he decided to stay on two feet in future instead of doing one of his famous front flip aerial somersaults. And the reason? He wanted to make sure he avoided any injury that would have meant him missing his fourth World

Cup with Germany. It worked, because Germany won that World Cup, in 2014, so Klose, who announced his retirement from international football after the tournament, ended with World Cup bronze (2006 and 2010), a silver (2002) and then that precious gold. Among his many other claims to fame was that he became the World Cup's all-time leading goalscorer with 16 goals. Perhaps even more importantly, and it's hard to find something more important than that, the Polish-born Klose also earned a deservedly wonderful reputation for honesty and fair play. He once refused to accept a penalty while playing for Werder Bremen as he felt the decision was wrong, and then told a referee he had handled the ball while scoring for Lazio. He explained: 'The referee asked me if I had touched the ball with my hand and it was not a problem for me to answer "yes". There are many youngsters who watch football on TV and we are role models for them.' Good old Miroslav.

He gets a mention now because he's a fellow German international, but Serge Gnabry's celebration has nothing more to do with this chapter than any in this book. Cooking might not be the first thing you think of when you want to come up with a trademark celebration but Gnabry took as his inspiration the American basketball star James Harden. The Houston Rockets player pretended to be cooking after scoring a crucial basket by imitating the flavouring and stirring of a dish. Gnabry took the celebration with him to Bayern Munich and told fcbayern.tv: 'So he was cooking, stirring it up, and that's the celebration.'

Russian international Andrei Arshavin will be best remembered at Arsenal for his finger-on-lips shushing gesture but on his return to his former club Zenit St Petersburg he celebrated a team-mate's goal in his first match back in a really weird way. As the colleague lay injured in the goalmouth, Arshavin stood on his stomach and then started to walk up his chest as well. Extraordinary.

It was Dutch legend Ruud Gullit who linked the s-word with soccer when he coined the phrase 'sexy football'. But to be fair, Roger Milla had already been there and got the t-shirt for sexiness on the football field. His official claim to fame is that when he scored for Cameroon in the 1994 World Cup against Russia, at 42 years old he became the oldest ever goalscorer in World Cup finals. But his other great gift to the beautiful game was his goal celebration. Jammed up close to a corner flag, he put one hand on his hip and wiggled suggestively and provocatively. Until his team-mates caught up to metaphorically throw a bucket of water over him.

Milla – his real name is Miller but he changed it to something more African-sounding – was named one of the 125 greatest living footballers by Pele. But his fame came late in a long career in the game. He'd retired from international football in 1987 and moved into peaceful semi-retirement on the idyllic-sounding Reunion Island in the Indian Ocean. But then he got a call from the President of Cameroon, Paul Biyau, asking him to join the national team for the 1990 World Cup in Italy. No pressure there on the team manager to put him in the team, once the country's president has summoned him, but Milla was actually only a substitute for each of his country's five games in the tournament. Their glorious run ended with a 3-2 quarter-final defeat by England, but by then Milla had scored four times and his legendary status had been established with his shimmying corner flag routine. In 2007 the Confederation of African Football named Roger Milla as the best African player of the past 50 years. And that celebration, since copied throughout the world by probably millions of players: 'It was totally spontaneous,' Milla said in a subsequent interview. 'I'd never done it before, not even in training.'

Corner flags weren't for sexy-dancing around when Lee Sharpe scored for Manchester United. His celebrations inevitably included some hip-shaking for the fans, but for something special he'd make a beeline for the corner, pluck out the flag, bend his knees, and do his very best Elvis impersonation with the flag post as his microphone. All shook up indeed.

Milla and Sharpe weren't the first footballers to race to the corner flag, though, according to ex-Wales international Jeremy Goss in his autobiography *Gossy*. He recalled: 'I'll never forget Keith Bertschin's goalscoring celebration of dancing round the corner flag. He was doing it long before Roger Milla and

Lee Sharpe made it fashionable. He loved scoring goals; he'd puff out his chest and stroll about the place as if he owned it.' Bertschin, an England under-21 international, played for a host of Football League clubs, scoring more than 100 goals in a career that lasted, despite plenty of injuries, until he was 41.

And while we're on the subject of corner flags getting involved in celebrations, as headbutts go it wasn't very violent, but Newcastle manager Alan Pardew still picked up a three-game stadium ban and a four-match touchline suspension for his overreaction and gentle headbutting move after a touchline squabble with Hull City's David Meyler in March 2014. What was much more violent was Meyler's re-enactment of the incident the following week after scoring against Sunderland in the FA Cup. He celebrated by giving the nearest corner flag a really fierce headbutt of his own – much to the delight of team-mates and cheering Hull fans.

Paolo Di Canio never failed to surprise, but when he volleyed the only goal of the game from close range for West Ham against Leicester in January 2002, he probably amazed himself with what happened next. He ran to the corner flag to celebrate, gave it a kick as he ran past, and didn't even notice as it rather forlornly snapped in two.

It's amazing what uses a corner flag can be put to, but Nathan Tyson discovered a new one when he celebrated Nottingham Forest's 3-2 win over close rivals Derby County in August 2009. At the end of the game, he grabbed a corner flag and waved it in front of the Derby fans. He was fined £5,000 and given a suspended ban, but that wasn't really why he regretted his actions. 'The whole flag-waving incident, I'm never going to live down,' Tyson told Sky Sports. 'That just shows how much passion is running through your veins. That night, I remember thinking, "Oh God, I'm going to get punished here." Which I did!'

Matt Ritchie has form for kicking corner flags, but he'd never previously hurt a fan until he celebrated Newcastle's injury-time winner against Chelsea on 18 January 2020. When Isaac Hayden scored a late goal he raced towards the Milburn Stand and was immediately followed by the ebullient Ritchie. The Scottish international took a mighty kick at the innocent corner flag and it spun into the crowd, hitting a Newcastle fan where it hurts most. While fans around him were jumping up and down, overjoyed at beating Chelsea, the poor man was doubled up in pain. Newcastle issued a public apology and the fan became a bit of a local celebrity for a short while – once he'd got his breath back.

It wasn't the first time a fan had been hit by a flying corner flag kicked by a celebrating player. John Carew scored the only goal of the game for Aston Villa against Stoke on 19 December 2009, but his spur-of-the-moment celebration ended with the flag hitting a seven-year-old fan. As chance would have it, the boy was wearing a Villa shirt with Carew's name on it, but the accident didn't put him off his hero worship. In fact, it worked the other way as the Norwegian striker immediately apologised and then went back after the game and gave the boy his shirt. So the youngster went home with two shirts sporting the name of Carew – who, incidentally, went on to a career in acting after his football days finished.

13

Tragedies: Dignified responses

POIGNANT AND respectful, Welsh international superstar Gareth Bale managed the most dignified of celebrations after scoring for Spurs against Bolton in 2011. Goal celebrations are all about exuberance and excitement, but Bale superbly managed the most difficult of challenges by turning a special moment into a personal tribute to his late international team manager.

At the time, Bale was a key member of the Wales team who were enjoying a huge resurgence under the inspired management of Gary Speed. Bale admitted to being shocked and devastated by Speed's untimely death on 27 November 2011 and the Spurs v Bolton match a week later was his first chance to pay his own respects in public. As Bolton was one of Speed's former clubs, it added extra significance to the occasion, and the match was preceded by a minute's applause in tribute to him.

But, ever the professional, Bale immediately got on with the game and the chance came early on as Luka Modric, who Bale later teamed up with at Real Madrid, played a low corner to the near post. The Welshman improvised a first-time flicked finish to beat Bolton keeper Jussi Jaaskelainen and put Spurs ahead. Bale then played out his pre-planned celebration in front of the applauding Bolton fans. He took off his left boot – Speed himself was notably left-footed – into which the words 'RIP Gary Speed' had been stitched and held it high above his head. 'It was a special moment and nice to be able to honour him in that way,' said Bale. 'It was my tribute to Gary and his family.' Spurs went on to win the match 3-0, their sixth successive league win at the time.

Just as special and moving was the celebration by Cardiff City's Bobby Decordova-Reid when he scored a fifth-minute penalty in his club's home match against Bournemouth on 2 February 2019. It was the first game Cardiff had played after the shocking death of striker Emiliano Sala when the plane he was travelling in on his way to Wales crashed into the sea. The Argentinian striker hadn't even had the chance to play for his new club but Cardiff had taken him to their hearts, and Decordova-Reid struck just the right mood with his goal celebration. He ran to the home team's bench and, surrounded by team-mates, held up a t-shirt with Sala's picture on it. There was hardly a dry eye in the house and even manager Neil Warnock, normally as tough as old boots, openly cried on the touchline after what was an amazing and emotional night.

It was a similarly touching moment when Josh Wright scored the only goal of the game for Leyton Orient as they beat Cheltenham on the opening day of the 2019/20 season. While pointing to the sky, he held up a shirt with the name of Justin Edinburgh on the back. Edinburgh was the much-loved manager of Orient, who at the end of the previous season had steered them to the championship of the Vanarama National League and back into the Football League after an absence of two years. Tragically, Edinburgh, a former Spurs defender, died following a cardiac arrest just over a month later, at the tender age of 49. And who was the last player he'd signed? None other than Josh Wright. And who is Wright's best mate? Justin Edinburgh's son Charlie. Wright had previously played under Edinburgh's management for Gillingham and became a close friend of the family then. 'To get the goal was extra special,' Wright said afterwards. 'The emotion is hard to explain. I could see Justin's family and friends up on their feet, going wild like Justin would have been up in the sky. It's something that will stick with me forever.'

It was watched by tens of thousands in the stadium, and by millions more on TV, but Frank Lampard's goal celebration in the second half of his illustrious career was for just one person. Lampard would isolate himself momentarily from team-mates to point up at the sky with both hands, a gesture he adopted following the untimely death of his mum Pat. She died in April 2008 at the tragically early age of 58 after developing pneumonia. Less than a week later, Lampard was back in action and, amid great emotion throughout the stadium, scored a penalty for Chelsea in their Champions League semi-final victory over Liverpool. He went on to play in his second and third World Cups for England and ended his playing career as Chelsea's all-time leading goalscorer. And in 2018 he and his TV presenter wife Christine had a baby daughter they named Patricia after his mum.

Why would any footballer risk a mandatory yellow card by removing their shirt to celebrate a goal? Well, sometimes the urge to be controversial, or even funny, is just too hard to resist. Andres Iniesta was motivated by something altogether different when he scored the winning goal for Spain in the 2010 World Cup Final. He took off his shirt to reveal a vest inscribed 'Dani Jarque: siempre con nosotros', which translates to 'Dani Jarque: always with us'. It was a tribute to a former team-mate who had died of a heart attack the previous year. English referee Howard Webb inevitably booked Iniesta, who still won the man-of-the-match award that day for his performance against Holland.

Emotions were obviously running high in the first match at Leicester City's King Power Stadium after the horrifying death of popular and respected club owner Vichai Srivaddhanaprabha in a helicopter crash in October 2018. Demarai Gray gave Leicester the lead against Cardiff and then revealed a t-shirt with the message: 'For You Vichai'. Referee Lee Probert got a lot of stick for booking Gray but, to be fair, rules are rules and he clearly did it with a heavy heart. After the game, Leicester's players and staff headed off on a 12,000-mile round trip to Thailand for Vichai's funeral.

It was a special moment at The Hawthorns on 20 January 2002 as West Bromwich Albion played Walsall the day after their legendary striker Jeff Astle died at the very early age of 59. Fittingly, it was a West Brom striker, Jason Roberts, who scored the only goal of the game and, even more fittingly, he celebrated by taking off his shirt to reveal a t-shirt with Astle's photo on it. Grenada international Roberts had a successful career with a number of clubs and was made an MBE for his services to sport, having set up a charity foundation to provide sporting opportunities for young people in the UK and Grenada.

Astle, nicknamed The King by West Brom fans, served the club for ten years, getting the only goal of the 1968 FA Cup Final, as well as playing five games for England. His goal celebration was always the same – a jump in the air, and a punch with his right fist, all the time a wide grin on his face. Sadly, he died at such a comparatively young age from a degenerative brain disease linked to consistently heading so many heavy and wet footballs.

Another player paying tribute to a special person in his celebration was Anthony Knockaert, when he scored for Brighton in a 3-0 win against Queens Park Rangers in December 2016, to put his team top of the

Championship. His celebration was dedicated to his late father Patrick. He waved team-mates away and, solemn-faced, ran to the touchline where someone on the bench passed him a framed picture of his dad. Anthony kissed it and held it up to the stands. He tweeted after the game: 'Nothing better to score for the main man in my life. Love you Daddy.'

Also paying tribute to his late father was Brentford's Said Benrahma, who revealed a t-shirt with the message 'I love you dad' in French after scoring an early goal away to Hull on 1 February 2020. The Algerian international got booked – of course – but battled on to complete a memorable hat-trick in a 5-1 win. Brentford manager Thomas Frank said: 'We all know it's very difficult when people lose a loved one. We gave him all the time off that he needed to get his head in the right place. He's had some emotional days but he said he wanted to play for his dad and it was a fantastic performance.'

It was a bitter-sweet moment, too, for Odion Ighalo when he scored in the first game he'd started for Manchester United after making his dream move to the club on loan from Chinese Super League side Shanghai Greenland Shenhua. The Nigerian striker put the ball over the line from close range as United beat Brugge 6-1 on aggregate in the Europa League on 27 February 2020. Ighalo slid towards the corner flag on his knees in the time-honoured way and then lifted his United shirt to reveal a white t-shirt with a picture of his late sister Mary and the date of her death. She had died suddenly in Canada a couple of months previously, and Ighalo said afterwards how sad it was that Mary hadn't seen him score for United as she was a big fan. He told MUTV: 'It is a bit emotional for me. I promise myself that every goal I score I will dedicate to her. She is up there watching me doing well for United.'

When Ighalo was previously in English football, playing for Watford, there was a lovely picture of him on his knees with his arms raised celebrating a goal against Liverpool in 2015. Beside him, Watford mascot Harry the Hornet has exactly copied his celebration. Ighalo turns to look at Harry as if he doesn't know whether to laugh or tell him to jog on.

Cheick Tiote scored a magnificent late equaliser for Newcastle in their 4-4 draw with Arsenal on 25 February 2011. His team had fought back from 4-0 down at half-time, Tiote capping the battling recovery with a swerving left-foot volley from outside the area to complete the biggest comeback in Premier League history. His celebration was special, racing back down the pitch to his own half with arms aloft, before diving forwards on to the turf. His team-mates piled on top of him, and goalkeeper Steve Harper added a comedy touch, with a neatly-executed clown-like fall to lay on the ground alongside his colleagues. But what a sad ending to the story, as Tiote tragically died of a cardiac arrest at the very young age of 30. His manager the day he scored the best goal of his life, Alan Pardew, hit the perfect note in tribute when he said Cheick was 'everything that you want in a Newcastle player'.

There's a memorial in a cemetery in Serbia depicting a footballer sliding on his knees to celebrate a goal. Dragan Mance was young, good-looking, and a proven goalscorer, when he was killed in a Belgrade road accident travelling to training on 3 September 1985. An estimated 20,000 people attended his funeral, and FK Partizan team-mates, in full black-and-white kit, carried the coffin. He was famous for his knee-slide celebration – many reckoned he even pioneered it – and the memorial at his grave was sculpted in an image of Dragan celebrating a goal he scored against Partizan's deadly rivals Red Star Belgrade the year before his death at the age of 23.

Going back to Bale, he was earmarked from an early age as having great potential and at 16 years and 315 days, he became the youngest player to represent Wales. He was eligible to play for England through his grandmother but his heart remained in the Welsh valleys. By the time in his career when he was scoring against Bolton and showing such maturity, he was still just a youngster of 22. But Bale had already been evolving what's become literally his trademark celebration.

When he scored for club or country he shaped his hands into a heart, a public gesture to Emma, his sweetheart since childhood. It became such an iconic celebration that, along with his squad number 11, Bale had it trademarked with the Intellectual Property

Office in June 2013, which means he can approve the use of the heart-handed logo on items such as clothing, footwear, headgear and jewellery. And, probably more lucratively, in the hugely successful online games market.

His love-heart celebration has been copied everywhere and anywhere throughout football, notably by ex-Real Madrid team-mate Angel Di Maria when he scored his first goal for Manchester United against QPR in September 2014. Though his tribute was apparently to highlight his love for football. Is romance dead?

Up till now, Bale has come out well in this chapter – a decent bloke, with love and respect for others. So he spoilt his goody-goody image a bit in February 2019 when he scored for Real Madrid against Atletico Madrid in La Liga. He then performed an Iberian Slap, which in many European countries is an offensive gesture. It's when you bend your arm into an L-shape with the fist pointing upwards, and then use the other hand to grip the biceps of the bent arm and force it upwards. Let La Liga's organising body explain: 'Bale lifted his right arm near his head in a clear sign of provocation towards the fans, then giving a gesture which could be seen as obscene and disdainful by folding his arm and striking it with his other hand.'

Stick to your love-heart, Gareth.

14

2019/20: A season to stick in the mind

THE PREMIER League season 2019/20 will be remembered for three special and unique reasons: Liverpool dominating it by a huge distance, the introduction of the controversial VAR system and the season's dramatic suspension in March because of the coronavirus.

First, the Video Assistant Referee system. All sorts of things went wrong with it, making it pretty frustrating all round for players, managers and the poor old, long-suffering, big-spending fans. For one thing, spectators were kept in the dark about what was happening. On top of that, some decisions being made remotely seemed to take forever. There was utter confusion over interpreting the new handball rule. Offside verdicts were being made on infinitesimally tiny amounts and that all became silly. The words 'clear and obvious' seemed to take on meanings that were neither clear nor obvious. And referees were told not to go and look at a pitchside monitor, even though the screens were seemingly there to be looked at.

Oh, and celebrations. They suffered too. It became ludicrous when a player couldn't celebrate for fear a colleague three passes back was offside by a toenail. And it's not a small thing – as we've learned from this book, celebrations are a massive part of the game and an enormous part of our enjoyment of it. If players stop doing them, or get to do a truncated version two minutes after the excitement has died down, our experience is diminished.

Right at the start of the season, Wolves manager Nuno Espirito Santo, talking about a long VAR delay before a decision was reached about whether a goal would be allowed, said: 'I didn't want to lose that moment. You celebrate a goal and it's such a beautiful moment. Don't take that away, it's the most important moment in football.'

Brighton's Leandro Trossard had a goal ruled out by VAR on his debut early in the season and the following week admitted it affected his reaction when his team seemed to have scored against Southampton. 'I knew not to celebrate after the previous week,' he told Sky Sports. 'I could tell something wasn't right.'

It was only a matter of time before VAR began to find its way into celebrations. Provocatively, but gently, with a good dash of humour.

Spurs had a goal ruled out by the Video Assistant Referee when Serge Aurier thought he had netted against Leicester in September 2019. So, when Tanguy Ndombele actually scored the following week in a home match with Southampton, the first person he looked for was Aurier. Between them they mimicked a referee calling up VAR, putting fingers to the ears, making a shushing gesture to those around them, and pretending they were drawing a large screen. There's a lovely picture of the two of them enjoying how clever they're being with a bemused-looking Harry Kane looking on as if he never got the email about what was being planned.

By coincidence, the Spurs duo weren't the only ones doing a bit of VAR point-scoring that afternoon. John McGinn had a goal for Aston Villa in their home match with Burnley correctly disallowed for offside, having been referred to the Stockley Park video experts, but he scored a legitimate goal later in the 2-2 draw. It was over in seconds but the message was very clear as McGinn ran off and pretended to call up VAR by shaping his fingers into a screen shape. Yes, John, we knew exactly what you meant.

Mind you, a certain Cristiano Ronaldo had beaten them to it as he mocked the new technology after scoring for Juventus in a 4-3 win over Napoli on 2 September 2019. He'd had a goal ruled out for offside by VAR the week before by the tiniest of margins. So when the superstar scored against Napoli he dropped his usual goal celebration and pretended to call for a video replay before gesturing for the crowd to wait calmly for an imaginary verdict.

Jonjo Shelvey made a telling if silent comment after scoring in a 2-0 win for Newcastle away to Sheffield United on 5 December 2019. Seeing the assistant referee raise his flag for offside, the Sheffield defenders stopped chasing Shelvey as he broke through on goal. Similarly, keeper Dean Henderson hesitated as he left his line and Shelvey kept cool to comfortably score past him. Once VAR had been invoked, it was ruled that the assistant referee had been wrong to flag and the goal was a good 'un. Before the season started, players had been told the game would only be stopped by the referee's whistle, and Shelvey was absolutely right to keep playing. He knew it, too, tapping the side of his head with his finger as he ran back. Message understood: he'd used his noddle and the Sheffield players hadn't followed instructions. Incidentally, when he's not pointing at his own head, Shelvey celebrates his goals by making a spectacles gesture. It's a bit of banter with his family, apparently, as they all wear glasses.

It's no coincidence that lots of the best celebrations during the season came from runaway leaders Liverpool. After all, so much of their success was down to teamwork, commitment and camaraderie, and their celebrations reflected that. And they also clearly got a lot of fun from taking the mickey out of each other.

Roberto Firmino is one of the biggest innovators and it's an ongoing in-joke that Sadio Mane copies his gestures. Even before the league season started he'd pointed out on Instagram that Mane was celebrating by using one of his moves. Mane said the boot was on the other foot, so to speak, and that Firmino was the one doing the copying.

Anyway, Firmino was in the thick of it again when he scored Liverpool's second goal in a 2-1 win over Chelsea early on in the season. He called over team-mate Virgil van Dijk and they impersonated a training ground pose Andrew Robertson had posted on Instagram. It showed him flexing his muscles while standing next to a bare-chested Mo Salah and commenting that it was just as well he'd kept his shirt on. Firmino and van Dijk found a handily-placed touchline camera to do their best impression of the hulk-like pose to keep the joke going.

It was Firmino and Mane who provided another laugh a couple of months later when van Dijk scored with two headers against Brighton. The Dutchman did his trademark jump celebration, kicking his legs and punching his right fist while still in mid-air. Running over to join the celebrations, Firmino and Mane took it in turns to exactly mimic the celebration, even though they'd played no part in the goals. Incidentally, van Dijk was caught on camera more than once during the season celebrating on the halfway line even before the shot on goal – usually by Mo Salah – had been taken.

Into January and Mane copied Firmino's double kung fu kick celebration when he scored against Sheffield United and the pair celebrated yet another win together. Firmino is one of the biggest goal celebrators football has known – he's had his shirt off many a time, and half off at others before seemingly thinking better of it. He's also executed dance moves, performed a somersault, imitated a matador, put his hand over one eye, used his fingers for pointed gun gestures, blown kisses, and shared funny handshakes with van Dijk. And those are just some of his celebrations.

High-scoring team-mate Mo Salah also has his favourite moves, including facing the crowd with his arms outstretched, and a yoga move where he stands on one leg with the other knee bent. But, also, he never forgets his roots and as a Muslim, he thanks Allah with a movement known as a sujud. It entails Salah going down on hands and knees and touching the ground simultaneously with his forehead, nose, both hands, knees and toes. He told CNN's *Inside the Middle East* programme: 'It's not kissing the ground. It's praying and saying thanks for what I have received. I've always done that since I was young, everywhere.'

James Milner, having built a reputation for being professional, sensible (even boring!), also got in on the fun with a goal celebration after he scored a penalty for Liverpool against Cardiff at the end of the previous season. He limped away in an impression of an old man using a walking stick. Apparently, it was in response to van Dijk's non-stop leg-pulling about his age. And what did the provocative van Dijk find so amusing about Milner's grand old age? Well, he was 33-and-a-quarter at the time of his goal, so judge for yourself. The routine wasn't original – Chelsea striker Samuel Eto'o posed as an old man after scoring against Spurs in a 4-0 win in 2014. He walked away, hunched like an OAP and holding his back, responding to his manager Jose Mourinho apparently suggesting Eto'o was 35 rather than his stated age of 32.

And to show that you can't keep a good Liverpudlian down, Harry Wilson scored from 25 yards for Derby against Manchester United in the Carabao Cup in September 2018 and raced off with five fingers raised. Why? Well, that represented Liverpool's five European Cups and young Wilson was a Liverpool player himself, on a season's loan to Derby. He wasn't the first to do it, Fernando Torres beating him to the high-five celebration after scoring for Liverpool against Manchester United at Old Trafford in 2009. Mind you, it's too late for anyone now as Liverpool made it six in 2019 and that's too many fingers for one hand.

Just to wrap it up with Liverpool, celebrations come in all shapes and sizes, and maybe it was just a coincidence but the wives of two of their players gave birth exactly nine months after the team's miraculous comeback to beat Barcelona in the previous season's Champions League climax. Both captain Jordan Henderson and striker Mo Salah became dads again in February 2020. And – another coincidence – both births were in the middle of Liverpool's two-week mid-season break, so the players weren't in danger of missing any games at the time. The victory over mighty Barcelona in May 2019 was in the semi-final of the Champions League, Liverpool sensationally turning the tables after trailing 3-0 from the first leg. Henderson was already the father to two daughters when wife Rebecca had a baby boy, while for Salah and his wife Maggi it was their second daughter.

After what seemed three particularly long months, top football returned in England in June 2020 following the suspension caused by coronavirus with Liverpool straightaway clinching the Premier League title for the first time ever. Socially distanced celebrations, or players told to head for a dedicated camera to show their delight, were much talked about during lockdown, but it was soon more of the same, though perhaps with a bit more restraint. There was fist-bumping, palm-slapping, badge-bashing, thumb-sucking, the ball stuck up the shirt (we knew then what had been going on in lockdown), and the occasional cuddle. And shouting. Players have always cheered themselves when they've scored but in empty stadiums now you heard them for all they were worth in the otherwise eerie silence. Meanwhile, taking the knee was totally adopted by footballers as a signal of support for the Black Lives Matter movement and solemnly used on occasions to celebrate a goal.

The Bundesliga in Germany had been the first big league to resume and Borussia Dortmund immediately proved their social awareness with a nicely-choreographed routine after Erling Haaland gave them the lead. Colleagues joined him in the corner for a little dance but strictly stayed more than two metres apart from each other. And again the players socially distanced at the end, making a spread-out line to run together towards the famous yellow wall (see page 61). Which, of course, was completely empty.

While Liverpool ended the 2010–19 decade as European and world champions, the two best players throughout that decade were indisputably Cristiano Ronaldo and Lionel Messi. They'd both won numerous *Ballon d'Or* awards as individuals, and Champions League titles with their clubs. Both have supreme skill and showmanship and both, of course, have instigated much-copied and hugely popular celebrations of their hundreds of goals.

Ronaldo has performed many different celebrations over the years but there's one which became a signature move. He would run towards the fans, jump high into the air, and then pirouette while he's up there. So he ends up landing with his back to the fans – but of course that means he's reminding them of his name, as well as facing his colleagues as they run to congratulate him. When his feet hit the ground, his hands are thrown down to his sides and his legs spread wide in a power stance. He then roars the word 'si', which is Spanish for yes. Ronaldo says it's a team shout, and, of course, all the crowd at the Bernabeu know to scream it with him when he does it.

Messi's trademark celebration is to point a finger on each hand to the sky as he goes back on his own to the halfway line, even if he's already celebrated with team-mates elsewhere on the pitch. It's to acknowledge his late grandmother Celia who encouraged the young Lionel to play football and took him to matches. *Mundo Deportivo* in Spain reported Messi as saying: 'I think about her a lot, I would have loved that she was here in the stadium, watching me, enjoying it. She gave us everything, myself and my cousins, she cared for all of us. I dedicate my goals and my triumphs to her.'

Other celebrations over the years by Ronaldo at Manchester United, Real Madrid and Juventus, as well as with the Portugal national team, and by Messi at Barcelona and with the Argentine national team, are:

Ronaldo: Squatting on his haunches with hands on his chin and looking thoughtful.

Messi: Showing a T-shirt in support of Fragile X Syndrome, a rare genetic condition.

Ronaldo: Pointing at himself or pointing to the stands.

Messi: Getting piggy-backs, or even the bumps, from team-mates.

Ronaldo: Finger to his lips and palms facing down.

Messi: Holding up his shirt to the crowd to show them his name.

Ronaldo: Mid-air jump collisions, or fancy handshakes, with team-mates.

Messi: Kissing the club badge.

Ronaldo: Both arms out horizontally.

Messi: Making the sign of the cross.

15

Posers: Milking
the moment

THE POSE. Fans must love it because they voted in their thousands for Eric Cantona as winner of the best goal celebration in the first 20 years of the Premier League. Playing for Manchester United against Sunderland on 21 December 1996, Cantona burst through from midfield, played a one-two with Brian McClair and without missing a beat scored with a beautiful chip beyond the keeper into the far corner. A sublime goal, and it needed a celebration to match. If anyone could provide it, Cantona was the man. He stood absolutely still, his face a picture of arrogance, pride and superiority. As he began to take on board the rapture of the crowd, the Frenchman slowly raised both arms with immaculate timing. No wonder he turned to acting after prematurely retiring from football.

Many years later, Cantona gave an interview to a United podcast and told them about that day. 'I never celebrate a goal in the same way, because every goal is different. The energy is different, everything is different,' he said. Cantona had briefly played alongside Lionel Perez, Sunderland's keeper that day, when they were together at Nimes in 1991. But when he went up to him in the tunnel before the game to shake his hand, Perez blanked him. Cantona continued: 'So maybe I scored this goal because of that! That's the biggest humiliation for a goalkeeper, and this kind of celebration too. Because he's angry and you don't run anywhere, I just stand there. Look at me.'

He won a medal for the best ever Premier League celebration and even then Cantona had a typically tongue-in-cheek response. 'That's the only thing I won? For a king like me it's not a lot!' he informed the Premier League's official website. Never anything but controversial, though also the scorer of some magnificent goals and the contributor of many wonderful memories, Cantona was voted Manchester United's greatest ever player by *Inside United* magazine. Beating superstars like George Best, Bobby Charlton, Ryan Giggs ... even for a king like him, that's quite, in his words, a lot.

Another player from the same club guilty of the occasional here's-one-for-the-camera pose was David Beckham, but as he is such a legend in his own lifetime, he's forgiven. I was at Southampton when England were playing Macedonia in a Euro 2004 qualifier. The players came out one-by-one for the warm-up to polite applause all round. Then, after a dramatic pause, out trotted Beckham and the roar that went up all round the ground could have been heard in Portsmouth.

Never was his pose more deserved than after scoring a wonderful goal for England to give them a 2-2 draw against Greece and earn a place in the 2002 World Cup finals. In front of his home Old Trafford crowd, Beckham hit a magnificent 25-yard free kick into the top corner. In his excitement he sprinted to the corner and then, after punching the air, threw both arms up, arching his back just slightly, to acknowledge the crowd. An iconic goal, given its timing, its importance, and its quality. But the celebration, not so much.

To be fair, it hadn't come on much since a previous Beckham wonder goal we've all seen many a time – from the halfway line for Manchester United away to Wimbledon on 17 August 1996 to make the final score 3-0. Spotting the home goalkeeper slightly off his line, the 21-year-old Beckham received a short pass from Brian McClair (that man again!) and took deliberate aim from fully 55 yards. The ball sailed over the keeper and into the net, and Beckham simply grinned, perhaps slightly sheepishly, with both arms raised high above his head. In his autobiography, *My Side*, he wrote: 'I couldn't have known it then, but that moment was the start of it all: the attention, the press coverage, the fame.' What helped him to all that ensuing attention and fame was a nifty bit of video-editing in the split second after the goal. When the camera turns to him, what Beckham actually does is spit on the ground. For posterity – thankfully – that moment's been edited out.

The thing about posing so imperiously after scoring a goal is that you have to be extraordinarily talented to get away with it. So step forward Thierry Henry and Brian Laudrup, two other players who have been revered by fans of the clubs they've represented so beautifully.

Henry scored more than 400 goals in a long and illustrious career, so had plenty of opportunity to think what looked best afterwards. Mostly, it was to look cool. The better the goal, the better the opposition, the more he'd learn to scale it down and just seem, well, composed. When he saw out his final playing days in the United States, he embellished that look by propping himself up against the goalpost, hand casually on hip, after a couple of goals for New York Red Bulls. Fans christened it 'Henrying' and in the internet-obsessed age, it soon went viral, with Henry photoshopped into propping up the leaning tower of Pisa or grabbing the ball from the cockerel on Spurs' club badge. Thierry himself shrugged it all off. 'There is nothing behind the celebration,' he told interviewers. 'I needed a rest. I saw the post and stopped by it. It's funny. That's all.'

When Arsenal erected a statue to Henry outside the Emirates Stadium in December 2011, it showed him celebrating a goal with a knee-slide – another of his trademark celebrations. Arsenal's all-time leading goalscorer and the only player to win the European Golden Boot for two successive seasons, Henry shed a few tears at the ceremonial unveiling of his statue, which stands alongside fellow legends Tony Adams and Herbert Chapman.

Henry emerged from his career as an Arsenal legend and Brian Laudrup enjoyed similar idolatry at clubs like Glasgow Rangers. It was a goal celebration for his country Denmark that's best remembered, though. He scored twice against Brazil in the 1998 World Cup quarter-final, and, for all their attacking pedigree, not many people score easily against them (apart from Germany in the 2014 semi-final, of course). But Laudrup did, thrashing the ball home inside the near post to make it 2-2 – though Brazil, who finished the tournament as runners-up, had the last word as they went on to nick it 3-2. When Laudrup scored he ran away, fell gracefully to the ground and lay there in beach-like pose, one hand casually propping up his head. It was so laid-back that Cantona or Henry would have been equally proud of it. All it needed to complete that picture was a sub running on to hand Laudrup his shades and a fruit-based cocktail.

Goalscorers in World Cup finals have often hurdled nearby advertising hoardings to celebrate goals. But not Gordon Strachan, even though he had plenty to jump about after putting Scotland 1-0 up against eventual finalists West Germany in the 1986 finals in Mexico. He hit an angled shot past German keeper Harald Schumacher and then raced to a nearby hoarding, bouncing up and down in excitement. But he's quite small, and the wooden hoarding comparatively high, and discretion became the better part of valour so instead of trying to jump it Strachan simply leant against it and raised his left leg to rest it rather nonchalantly on top and survey his surroundings. As cool as you like, he then just waited there for team-mates to arrive to congratulate him. The ebullient Strachan retired from playing in 1997 at the age of 40, which was a Premier League record for an outfield player.

Never has a footballer been so lampooned for celebrating a famous victory. In fact he liked it so much he did it twice. And never has so much mockery – some good-willed and some not so much – been like water off a duck's back. That's John Terry for you. What he did was accept the trophy on Chelsea's behalf after they'd won the Champions League Final in 2012, beating Bayern Munich on penalties. He looked immaculate in the traditional Chelsea blue kit as he lifted the huge trophy and posed for photographs.

The controversy was, he hadn't actually played in the match because of suspension and had changed into his playing kit for the presentation ceremony. No wonder he looked immaculate. The internet-led banter that followed saw Terry super-imposed behind Bradley Wiggins on his bike, joining Andy Murray as he lifted a trophy, and even accompanying Neil Armstrong walking on the moon.

Did he mind? Well, not at all, as his response was to do it again the following year. This time he missed the Europa League Final because of an ankle injury, but still came out in full kit at the Amsterdam Arena to lift the trophy. Terry himself later explained that he felt a huge part of what Chelsea achieved at the time, and that his team-mates thought the same and wanted him to share the celebrations.

Alan Shearer scored 260 Premier League goals before retiring in 2006, but the ex-England captain is still a legend at Newcastle, where a huge statue of him is proudly on display. There was slight controversy when it was unveiled at St James' Park as it shows Shearer celebrating with his customary right-arm salute but with his index finger pointing rather than flat-handed. Pictures clearly show him with his hand in either position, and his finger was in the air when celebrating his final Newcastle goal, a penalty in a 4-1 win over local rivals Sunderland in April 2006.

Billy Bremner, voted Leeds United's greatest player of all time in a 2006 poll, will forever be celebrating a goal outside the club's Elland Road ground with arms raised and fists clenched. He's immortalised in a nine-foot bronze statue created by Leeds-born sculptor Frances Segelman, who worked for two solid and devoted years on her masterpiece. She spent a lot of time with his widow – Bremner himself died of a heart attack at the young age of 54 – and studied every detail of his life on and off the field, including how his musculature worked during a game.

Mind you, what's the only thing sadder than not having a goal-celebration statue erected outside the club you've dedicated years of your successful career to? Well, it's got to be having one built and then fans tearing it down when you join one of their rivals. Gabriel Batistuta was a great celebrator of the many goals he scored in a successful career for both club and country – perhaps that was one of the main reasons Fiorentina fans worshipped him enough to honour him with a statue in 1996. The life-size bronze was styled on one of his favourite goal poses. He ran to the corner flag, grabbed it out of the ground, and stood screaming. Inscribed on the statue was a legend which translates as: 'He is a warrior who will not surrender, who is hard in the fight but is fair in the soul.' Not only was he a warrior-star in his playing days for the Italian club, he also showed loyalty, which is not a given with every modern footballer. When Fiorentina were relegated to Serie B in 1993 on goal difference, Batistuta, who'd been one of the top goalscorers throughout Italy that season, stuck with them and helped the club climb straight back up again.

The Argentinian played for Fiorentina for nine seasons, spurning offers from clubs like Manchester United and Barcelona, yet never won the Italian League with them despite being their all-time record goalscorer. He joined Roma in 2000 for what was a record transfer fee paid for a player over 30 and rectified the gap on his CV with a Serie A title. But when he scored against his much-loved former club he not only refused to celebrate but he had a tear in his eye, too. Somewhere along the way his statue disappeared from outside Fiorentina's Stadio Artemio Franchi, but Batistuta's legendary status at the club was confirmed when he was inducted into their hall of fame 14 years after leaving. Again tears were shed as he told them: 'From the moment I arrived at Fiorentina I wanted a place in the history of the club – and now I can say I have succeeded.'

And what of the other goal celebrations made famous by Batistuta, described by no less a legend than Diego Maradona as the best striker he's ever seen? He knew the perfect celebration after silencing Barcelona's mighty Camp Nou in 1997 with a great right-footed volleyed goal from the edge of the box. He ran away, span around, took in the moment and shushed the crowd with his finger on his lips. He showed his versatility in the celebration stakes by also pioneering the machine gun, going down on one knee and pretending to silence the opposition fans by mowing them down.

As we've seen, for some special players a golden moment in their career may be enshrined in a statue. For Kevin Phillips, who after all is the only Englishman to have won the European Golden Shoe trophy, having scored 30 goals for Sunderland in the Premier League in 1999/2000, it's a mural. Phillips netted a crucial goal against Wolves to help West

Bromwich Albion reach the Championship play-off in 2007, and Baggies fans voted it as their most iconic moment of all time. Courtesy of an awareness campaign by the charity Mind, the smartly-painted mural of Phillips celebrating his goal now graces a side wall in West Bromwich's indoor market.

Another celebration was based on a statue, rather than a statue being based on the celebration. Brilliant Brazilian striker Ronaldo often marked his goals by running at full tilt with both arms outstretched. The celebration was a copy of the iconic Christ the Redeemer statue which stands high above Ronaldo's native Rio de Janeiro. It was in 1997, when he was World Footballer of the Year, that Ronaldo repeated his celebration for a Pirelli advertising campaign. The company announced: 'In a highly spectacular picture, Ronaldo embodies a strong sense of power and dominion provided by his miraculous feet, transformed, on this occasion, in Pirelli tyres.' So now you know.

A few years later, Ronaldo was named the world's most famous sportsperson in a poll conducted by Nike, and it's probably pure coincidence that when he was at Inter Milan, team-mates often celebrated his goals by kneeling down and pretending to shine his boot. A Nike one, of course.

His Brazilian superstar colleague Kaka has other claims to fame apart from his football at which he was a World Cup winner. He was reckoned to be the first sportsman to amass 10 million followers on Twitter, and in 2004 he also became the youngest ambassador of the United Nations' World Food Programme. And his goal celebration? Kaka would point to the sky as a gesture of thanks to God.

And finally in this chapter, why shouldn't referees celebrate if they get a decision right and it leads to a goal? Well, experienced Premier League ref Mike Dean has been suspected of doing exactly that. He raised both arms to signal he was giving a player the advantage when Spurs were attacking against Aston Villa in November 2015. This led to a goal and Dean kept his arms up rather too long after the ball had gone in, as if he was pleased with himself at how his advantage decision had worked out.

It's a knockout as boxing fan Wayne Rooney scores for Manchester United against Spurs and re-enacts an image that ended up on the front page of a national newspaper. (Getty Images)

A moment of madness as Brandi Chastain celebrates after scoring the winning penalty for USA in the 1999 Women's World Cup. (Getty Images)

I told you so: Jimmy Bullard lectures Hull City team-mates as a celebration of his successful penalty at Manchester City. (PA Images)

Love you: Gareth Bale demonstrates his trademark loveheart celebration after scoring for Spurs away to Aston Villa. (Getty Images)

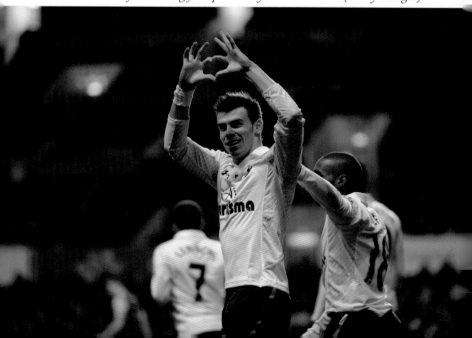

Sergio Aguero celebrates the moment that Manchester City won the Barclays Premier League in 2012 with his late winning goal against QPR. (Getty Images)

Having the last word as Liverpool's Craig Bellamy celebrates a Champions League goal at Barcelona with one of his golf swings. (Getty Images)

Typical Klopp. Liverpool manager Jurgen Klopp doesn't hold back with his celebration as he enjoys victory over Leicester City at Anfield. (Getty Images)

An iconic picture as Roger Milla dances with a corner flag after scoring for Cameroon against Colombia in the 1990 World Cup in Naples. (Getty Images)

Ellen White has goals in her sights as she performs her goggles celebration especially for her husband, as well as her England teammates, in a Wembley friendly. (Getty Images)

A mixed reaction from the Crystal Palace fans as Jamie Vardy pretends to be an eagle after scoring against them for Leicester City. (Getty Images)

A moment to remember for Ian Wright as he celebrates breaking the Arsenal goalscoring record set by Cliff Bastin. (Allsport)

You never lose it: Robbie Keane turns back time with one of his old celebrations after scoring for Spurs Legends in 2019. (Getty Images)

Showing just how much it means to the fans – David Beckham runs to the Manchester United supporters after scoring a goal. (Getty Images)

Defiant Raheem Sterling challenges the crowd in Podgorica after enduring racist abuse when England beat Montenegro in a 2020 European Championships qualifier. (Getty Images)

I made it, you scored it: Goalkeeper Alisson ran the length of the field to congratulate Mo Salah after his goal for Liverpool against Manchester United on their way to the 2019/20 Premier League championship. (Getty Images)

16

Dance: Like nobody's watching

WHAT HE really wanted to be famous for was scoring the goals for England that won the World Cup. Instead Peter Crouch will forever be associated with his 'RoboCrouch' celebrations that provoked mass media hysteria in 2006. Like so many of the best celebrations, he was taking the mickey out of himself. The 6ft 7in Crouch had been filmed dancing at a party at David Beckham's house, and his on-the-pitch celebration was a parody of that moment. He introduced it after scoring for England against Hungary that summer, spinning backwards with his arms tucked in and hands pointing upwards in robot-style movements. That description doesn't it do justice but in the frenzy of a World Cup build-up we all went crazy for it.

Despite admitting that he was only ever a Plan B for England, Crouch had an impressive goalscoring record for his country, but the abiding memory of his career will always be of his exceptional height, and that crazy dance. Crouch himself ditched the celebration at just the right time, before we all got fed up with it. 'It's not about robotic dancing – it's about scoring goals and winning matches,' he said. He promised we'd never see it again, unless in special circumstances such as winning the World Cup or the Champions League Final. And those boats have sailed by now for the loveable Crouch.

But, as we know, promises are made to be broken and there's a PS to this story. On 1 February 2016, Crouch scored his 100th Premier League goal – in Stoke City's 1-1 draw with Everton – and guess what was wheeled out of retirement? It happened 15 years after he scored his first Premier League goal, and it had taken him 419 games to reach the milestone. And the robot celebration? 'It was a bit of nostalgia, pulling it out,' said Crouch, who at 36 years and two days became the oldest man to reach 100 Premier League goals. 'It was a bit stiff to be honest and I think I'll definitely have to retire it. Weddings and parties only now.'

Crouch devotes a whole chapter to goal celebrations in his entertaining 2018 book *How to be a Footballer*. Impressed by the way Eric Cantona celebrated by looking like a gladiator in an arena, Crouch wrote: 'I always thought if I scored a worldie I would stand there with my arms by my side and turn to all corners of the ground and let them salute me. The coolest man in the stadium, the coolest kid in town. But when I scored my flick-up and volley against Manchester City in 2012, I instead lost it. First, I started shouting, "I've scored a worldie, I've scored a worldie!" Then I ran around for a bit with my hand over my mouth. Then I ran around for a bit longer. Kissed my hand and waved it at a television camera, jumped in the air and disappeared under a pile of team-mates.'

A reminder of that story came in the rather unexpected quarters of the BetVictor Northern Premier League on a wet and windy Tuesday night in Manchester in October 2019. Stefan Galinski was playing centre-back for Basford United away to FC United when he got a nice defensive header in to a clearance from the opposition keeper. So nice, it carried 60 yards, bouncing and skidding over the poor keeper and straight into the goal. The extraordinary moment's been seen by millions on social media, but it was so out of the blue, Stefan's celebration was a bit, well, muted. All he could think of doing was running to the corner flag while shouting: 'I've scored a fucking 60-yard header.' Crouchie would have been proud of him.

Jesse Lingard puts a lot of effort and creativity into his goal celebrations. They're enthusiastic, imaginative, well-planned, show off his considerable dancing skills and are very much in the moment and topical. But the Manchester United and England player revealed in an interview with Sky Sports that there's a purpose to it all, too. He said: 'I like to celebrate my goals. You know young fans are watching and I might just inspire one or two to go and play football, to see them dancing, you know it's good to get kids active. Most kids these days are on their iPad and iPhone, you rarely see kids in the street kicking a football anymore. So you've gotta be that inspiration for youngsters to get out there and play.'

Lingard has his own unique celebration, which he filed with the UK Intellectual Property Office so he can use it as a logo on clothing and footwear. He turns his hands towards his body, puts out his thumbs and raises the index finger on each hand, so he spells out his initials JL. He and his mate Marcus Rashford came up with it and they tried to plan one for each of them but couldn't figure out how to get a letter R. Apart from that, Lingard has celebrated goals with a Milly Rock celebration, a special dance used on the *FIFA 19* and *20* games which saw him nominated for a Nickelodeon Kids' Choice Award; the Michael Jackson Moonwalk, which he performed at Arsenal after scoring there; the Shmoney dance made famous by American rapper Bobby Shmurda; the dance craze Dab which Paul Pogba partners him in; the Wakanda dance from the *Black Panther* film; the Shoot or Hype dance popularised by the video game *Fortnite*; another from an American rapper, this time BlocBoy JB; and the 'stoopid challenge' craze which emanated from social media. Oh, and Lingard also had a celebration where he pretended to play a flute while dancing a jig. That, he told MUTV, was because he promised a friend he would pay tribute to a new Drake track called 'Portland' if he scored.

Perhaps because he couldn't work out how to do an R, Rashford is most likely to go in for an enthusiastic knee-slide as well as immediately look for someone else to share his enjoyment with. As an 18-year-old, he made his Manchester United debut in a Europa League match at Old Trafford in February 2016 against Danish side FC Midtjylland, after Anthony Martial pulled out injured in the warm-up. Rashford scored twice and rushed to the part of the crowd where players' friends and family sit where he was embraced by his mate from the youth team, goalkeeper Dean Henderson. Bet they weren't even thinking about how in a few years' time they'd be in the England squad alongside each other. Rashford's knee-slide was suspected of possibly causing him an injury after a spectacular long-range free-kick goal against Chelsea in November 2019, but United manager Ole Gunnar Solskjaer didn't believe the slide was to blame and said his players were free to celebrate goals in whatever way they wanted. The boss had been there himself, as he injured his own knee with a triumphant slide after scoring United's dramatic winning goal in the 1999 Champions League Final.

He just about gets away with it because he's cute-looking, but probably one day French star Antoine Griezmann might look back at his advert for Puma deodorants and feel just a little bit embarrassed. It was based on his goal celebration known as Hotline Bling after a music video by Drake (again) and involves the French star grinning while giving a double thumbs-up to the nearest camera. The Puma people built a series of scenes for their ad which all end with Griezmann helping men make themselves more appealing to the woman they're trying to attract. Perhaps a bit 20th century, that one, for some tastes.

The online video game *Fortnite* couldn't have had a higher profile than Griezmann doing a dance from it in the 2018 World Cup Final. The Barcelona player gave France a 2-1 lead in the decisive win over Croatia, on his way to a man-of-the-match performance, and he celebrated with a *Fortnite* move. He performed the Take The L dance, which involves making the letter L with your fingers and splaying your legs sideways in a rhythmic dance. Dele Alli also did a *Fortnite* dance during that World Cup, having scored for England in their quarter-final match with Sweden. His celebration was pretending to ride a pony while swinging both arms.

Going back a few World Cups, and talking of dancing, Rio Ferdinand let his hair down metaphorically after scoring his first England goal. It was early in the round of 16 match against Denmark in the 2002 World Cup and set England on the way to a 3-0 win. In *Rio My Story*, Ferdinand describes the moment: 'I did a little dance to celebrate and every time I see it on video I get more embarrassed. I look like a man possessed. The emotion on my face is a mixture of joy, anger and relief.' There was a bit more of all those emotions after the match when Garth Crooks, interviewing Rio for the BBC, told him there was talk of it being given as an own goal by the Danish goalkeeper. Ferdinand recalls: 'I swore my head off saying, "It's fucking my goal, man."'

Michelle Obama did it. So did Adele and Beyonce. And so did Jamie Vardy. The mannequin challenge was a short-lived – thankfully! – social media craze in November 2016 that took the US, and then the rest of the world, by storm. The idea was for the central figure to freeze, often in the middle of an elaborate pose, while the camera keeps on moving through the surroundings. Vardy took up the challenge after scoring for England in a friendly against Spain at Wembley. As he turned away to acknowledge the goal, he suddenly stood stock still, staring straight ahead with his arms half-outstretched. Behind him, colleagues Raheem Sterling and Theo Walcott, clearly in on what was going to happen, also stopped mid-celebration.

It was clever and funny because spectators, and millions watching at home, hadn't seen it coming. And more than that, the TV broadcasters were caught by surprise and thought their coverage had frozen. All sorts of football teams got in on the act by doing their own version of the mannequin challenge – including Spain later in the same match. And those likely lads of any trendy trend, Manchester United and England pair Jesse Lingard and Marcus Rashford – haven't we just met them? – also got involved with an amusing internet post.

Don't take your eyes off Paul Pogba if a goal's scored. He loves the attention and limelight, that moment when all eyes are on him. He's won the World Cup with France, scoring in the final against Croatia in 2018 with a left-foot drive after his initial shot was blocked, but by Pogba standards his celebration was nothing special. Arms spread wide, he raced to the corner flag where he was engulfed by all his colleagues and a bench full of substitutes in a huge pile-on. Normally, he's got a dance move up his sleeve, or something pre-planned with a team-mate.

Much more light-hearted was his famous Dab celebration, which originated in the USA and is based on a dance move from the Atlanta hip-hop scene, the dancer dropping his head while raising his left arm and right elbow. He introduced it while playing for Juventus and then brought it to Manchester United for his second stay at Old Trafford. Somewhat bizarrely, Pogba's Dab was used in a maths test for French students. An accompanying graphic on the question papers showed Pogba performing the Dab, with a triangle drawn over each of his arms. Students were asked to calculate whether the squared length of each triangle's longest side was equal to the length of each triangle's other two sides when they were squared and then added together. No, we didn't understand the question either – answers on a postcard please.

No sooner were Dab imitators all over the world trying to copy Pogba, than he announced he had dropped it in favour of the Billy dance, named after a childhood friend. He introduced that one, hopping from foot to foot and swaying his hips, after Manchester United beat Ajax 2-0 to win the Europa League in 2017.' 'I will make sure that everyone does it,' Pogba said. 'I'll make sure that it goes on *FIFA 18*!'

Since then he's performed a variety of other celebrations, including the baby-rocking routine on one occasion, a Cantona-like stock-still pose after a particularly striking goal, a political protest about Libya, as we saw earlier, and a variety of different dance moves. And Pogba makes no excuses: 'Everybody knows I love to dance. That is how I celebrate my goals.'

Another player who likes a dancing celebration is Antonio Rudiger – even when he's injured and on crutches. The Chelsea defender was very high-profile on the pitch at Baku after his team-mates had clinched the 2019 Europa League by beating Arsenal and didn't let an injury spoil some of his moves. And he introduced fans to the viral dance craze 'the Woah' after scoring against Leicester in the Premier League on 1 February 2020. Without crutches, obviously. For the uninitiated, it involves making a quick, small circular motion with the fists and leaning into a freeze position when the beat drops in the song.

Not sure what the odds would have been on the composer Khachaturian getting a name-check in this book, but he's made it. Fair play to him. An Armenian, he wrote the 'Sabre Dance' and that music was played over the PA at Shakhtar Donetsk whenever ex-Manchester United and Arsenal player Henrikh Mkhitaryan scored. The Ukrainian club had the tradition of playing music by someone from the scorer's country and Mkhitaryan is Armenian, too.

He's got long, slightly straggly blond-tinted hair like a surfer. And he did a surfing imitation when he scored against Premier League reigning champions Manchester City in September 2019. But Norwich City's Todd Cantwell has never been surfing in his life. His celebration, he explained to former Norwich striker Chris Sutton in an interview for the *Daily Mail*, wasn't planned at all. It's just that Cantwell had been watching music videos on his phone before the game and one of the songs was 'Surf' by an American rapper, Young Thug. 'As soon as I scored, it just happened,' he explained.

Talk about a dream start, but Steven Bergwijn scored a terrific goal on his Spurs debut with his first ever shot in the Premier League. It set them on the way to a 2-0 win over reigning champions Manchester City on 2 February 2020, and it was a great climax to his first week at the club after signing in a big-money move from Dutch club PSV. His big moment came in the 61st minute, chesting the ball down on the edge of the area before hitting a perfect volley into the far corner past City keeper Ederson. His celebration was oven ready, as he covered his face with one hand and crossed two of his fingers. Which is not quite as easy as it sounds. Asked to explain afterwards what it meant, Bergwijn said: 'It's nothing special, it has just come from when I play *FIFA* with friends. They said "do it like this" and since then I have always done it like this.'

Soon after his wonder goal, Bergwijn – 'When I saw the ball go in I almost cried!' – went down with cramp and had to be substituted. But he was on the far side of the field at the time and had to go off there, at the nearest point. So he had to hobble halfway round the ground to get back to the bench and, as luck would have it, Spurs scored again when he was limping behind the goal. Safe to say it was quite a moment with their delighted new player in touching distance of thousands of delirious fans celebrating up close and personal.

It doesn't get much better than a congratulatory tweet from Hollywood legend Dwayne 'The Rock' Johnson, so it was a proud moment for Wycombe Wanderers' striker Adebayo Akinfenwa – a bit of a legend himself – when that particular message pinged on to his phone. Akinfenwa scored twice in a 3-2 win over Port Vale in August 2017 and celebrated his second with an expertly executed WWE move. His team-mate Luke O'Nien lay on the ground and Akinfenwa dropped down beside him. Known as the People's Elbow, it's a routine straight from The Rock's playbook, and the man himself, now a film star, was full of praise for Adebayo's technique. 'Heart stoppin' elbow droppin' … well done brotha' was what Dwayne tweeted to him.

Victor Moses liked a good somersault or two when he played in England but when he went on loan from Chelsea to Turkey he celebrated his maiden goal for Fenerbahce by paying tribute to fictional superhero Batman. He told Fenerbahce TV: 'The celebration is basically when Batman is on a mission, you can't see him, so that's what it is obviously.' Perhaps it lost a bit in the translation.

Born in Dublin with Nigerian parents and brought up in London, Michael Obafemi had a choice when it came to a chance to play international football. The Southampton striker decided on the Republic of Ireland and when he made his debut he became the first player born in the 21st century to turn out for them. His goalscoring celebration reflected his choice, with a performance of a neat little Irish jig. Michael Flatley would be proud of him.

Someone who's always seemed to be a serious, grown-up, no-nonsense international footballer pinched a celebration from an unlikely source. When Phil Jagielka scored with a diving header for Everton against Wigan in 2011, he broke out the dance from *The Inbetweeners Movie*. Though to be fair to Jagielka, he did it better than the lads in the film. He raced across to the touchline, where restaging the dance involved lifting his elbows up very high and jiggling around a little bit. *The Inbetweeners* was a cult classic for teenagers, and the fans seemed to love Jagielka's attempt to get down with the kids. He explained: 'I made a pact with Tim Cahill that if he scored I'd back him up and if I scored he'd back me. I'll have to look at the video to see if he did. Otherwise I look like a plonker.' No worries, Jags, it's all been checked out and Cahill was with you in the thick of the celebrations.

Just a mention of Tim Cahill and most can recall him pugnaciously taking on a corner flag after scoring for Everton or his native Australia. For years, starting in 2005, scoring a goal would immediately mean running to the corner for Cahill. There he would pretend to aggressively trade punches with the flag, all the while clutching the badge on his club shirt between his teeth. It was apparently inspired by a kung-fu celebration a fellow Australian international used to do and he told Cahill he was welcome to adapt it for the Premier League. As well as his punching outbursts, Cahill once dedicated a goal to people affected by bushfires back in Australia, and another time mimed rowing a canoe in honour of people in Samoa affected by an earthquake and tsunami. But yet another dedication got him into trouble. That was in 2008 when he held up his crossed hands as if they were handcuffed after scoring against Portsmouth. It was a tribute to his brother, who had recently been jailed. Afterwards, he apologised and said it was a spontaneous and emotional gesture intended solely to show his brother he was thinking of him.

Ipswich's David Norris also made the handcuffs gesture after scoring in a game at Blackpool in November 2008, intending to show his support for a friend who had been imprisoned for causing the deaths of two young boys while drunk-driving. He was fined £25,000 by his club and personally apologised to the parents of the children for his ill-judged celebration.

He wasn't the first to do it (Roma's Francesco Totti beat him to it by taking a selfie in 2015) and he won't be the last. But Mario – Why Always Me? – Balotelli inevitably stole the limelight when he posted a celebration straight on to Instagram after scoring for Marseille in 2019. He grabbed a phone from a photographer behind the goal, and after sending the image of his smiling face he carried on playing as his team beat Saint-Etienne 2-0. The Italian international came up with something else original the following week when he scored the only goal of the game against his old club Nice and sat down on the grass to play rock-paper-scissors with team-mate Florian Thauvin. To say his former colleagues were not amused by his antics is a bit of an under-statement.

Young readers won't believe this, but once upon a time there were no selfies, no Instagram, no social media at all. So we relied on newspaper photographs, occasional TV coverage, and word of mouth to spread the news if somebody had an original goal celebration that was worth sharing. Oh, and there were postage stamps. That was one of the ways images of the officially recognised Player of the Century celebrating one of his goals were seen by a wider audience.

Pele was the youngest goalscorer in the World Cup finals when he netted for Brazil on their way to winning the 1958 tournament. He also won two more World Cups in a career of more than 1,300 games, and a celebration of a goal he scored at the Maracana stadium in Rio De Janeiro was commemorated on one of the many stamps issued in honour of the great man – not just by Brazil, but by many countries around the world, all of them in awe of not just his ability but his enduring dignity and personality as well. Pele's most iconic goal celebration was in the final of the 1970 World Cup when he headed Brazil into the lead against Italy. They went on to win 4-1 and Pele's goal was a landmark, the 100th scored by Brazil in World Cups. In celebration, a hugely delighted Pele leapt into the arms of team-mate Jairzinho and held the pose, punching the air with his arm. What a photo that moment made.

It may not be an egg-cellent celebration, but Kevin Nolan stayed loyal to his chicken impression through a career that involved captaining Bolton, Newcastle and West Ham. Basically, he flapped his arms and ran around like a chicken – a celebration that had its roots over a few beers with the boys on a summer break in Marbella. Nolan said: 'It's called a "quack". When we go away every year, the lads decide what celebration I'm going to do and they picked that one, so I've got to do it. But one of the lads actually dances like that, so you can imagine what he looks like on a Saturday night!' Sunderland fans had an amusing song for Nolan when he failed to score against them while playing for West Ham: 'Your chicken is dead, Your chicken is dead, Kevin Nolan, Your chicken is dead.'

Jamie Vardy – we've met him before in this chapter – looked as if he might be attempting Kevin's chicken dance when he scored Leicester City's late second goal in a 2-0 win at Crystal Palace on 3 November 2019. Confronting Palace fans who had been in the centre of taunts about his wife Rebekah, Vardy flapped his arms about and did a skipping run like children used to do when they were pretending to ride a horse. He finished the brief celebration with a huge and satisfied grin. So was it a chicken? Or a horse? It might not have been immediately obvious, but of course it was actually an eagle. Hitting the Palace fans where it hurts.

17

Shirtless: Tearing off a strip

BACK IN the day, taking your shirt off wasn't a problem yellow card-wise so Diego Forlan was quite happy to strip off after scoring a cracking winner from outside the box for Manchester United against Southampton in November 2002. Only problem was, the Uruguayan international hadn't put it back on when the game restarted. So clutching his shirt in his hand, he ran around bare-chested, tracking back and trying to make a tackle. Incidentally, he had quite a good body to show off, too. Forlan, who had only been on the field as a substitute for a few minutes when he scored his goal, told the South American press: 'The goal was one of the best ones I have done in my career. So I went to the corner where the parents of the players always are and I dedicated my goal to my brother and a couple of friends. The only problem was I couldn't get my shirt back on but I had to keep on playing.'

Diego's wasn't even the best bare-chested celebration Manchester United fans had ever seen – number one belongs to Ryan Giggs, with one of the most iconic of all time. The goal that preceded the celebration had something to do with that, as Giggs dribbled past five players in a run from his own half before smashing the ball past David Seaman to win a 1999 FA Cup semi-final replay against Arsenal at Villa Park. Understandably, he went a bit potty and twirled his white United shirt around his head while dashing bare (and hairy) chested along the touchline. He admitted: 'I don't know where that came from or why I did it! It was one of those out-of-body experiences. I'd decided during the game the next time I got the ball I was going to have a little dribble and it wasn't until I watched it again that I realised I had beaten that many men.'

It took 50 years for Cliff Bastin's record of 178 goals for Arsenal to be overtaken by the legend that was Ian Wright. So what if he was just a few minutes out with his celebration. He'd been wearing an undervest inscribed '179 Just Done It' for a few weeks on the off-chance that he'd break the record that day. So, when he scored at Highbury against Bolton Wanderers on 13 September 1997 up came his red-and-white Arsenal shirt to reveal the claim. Unfortunately, he'd forgotten it was only goal number 178. But the opportunity came just five minutes later, and it was so easy even his mum, watching from the stands, could have scored it. He followed up after a

Dennis Bergkamp shot was blocked and simply had to roll the ball over the line from a yard out. This time it was for real and Wright set off for a celebration sprint with his shirt over his head and the 'Just Done It' logo on show for the whole stadium to see. Wright recalled later to the BBC: 'When I scored the first time I was so excited I thought I'd broken the record, which is why I showed off the vest at the wrong time. People have not forgotten that one! Fortunately, I only had to wait a few more minutes before I did it for real, with one of the easiest goals I have ever scored. I went on to complete a hat-trick so I came off very happy and completely drained emotionally to mark what was a brilliant day.'

Thierry Henry broke that record a decade later but Wright reacted with dignity when he found out: 'It was amazing to have that record and it took a World Cup winner, a Champions League winner – one of the all-time greats – to take it away from me.'

Footballers over the years have always run the risk of getting in trouble by displaying messages on t-shirts or vests, though often it's been something as innocent as to celebrate the birth of a new baby or boast about passing some sort of record. But that hasn't stopped all sorts of players displaying messages, including: Why Always Me? (Mario Balotelli at Manchester City); Keep Calm and Pass Me The Ball (Dimitar Berbatov at Fulham); Shit On The Villa (Paul Tait at Birmingham); Happy New Year (Edin Dzeko at Manchester City); God is Great (Steven

Pienaar at Everton); and Watford's Danny Graham, whose under-shirt revealed he was the club's table tennis champion!

It all went slightly pear-shaped for Everton's Richarlison when he rolled out a goal celebration after scoring against Lincoln in the 2019/20 Carabao Cup. The idea was to channel the great Lionel Messi, who'd taken off his shirt and held it up to display his name and number to Real Madrid fans after scoring against them for Barcelona in a 2017 El Clasico encounter. Richarlison didn't get it quite right, though, as he held the shirt the wrong way round, with his name and number facing him rather than the fans.

The thumb-suck was just one of the many celebrations Serbian international Aleksandar Mitrovic tried out, and that was as he approached the arrival of a new baby at home. But his best – and funniest – celebration was after his powerful far-post header gave Newcastle a 1-1 draw with their oldest rivals Sunderland on 20 March 2016. Not just ignoring his team-mates, but physically brushing them aside, he immediately stripped down to his bare chest and ran off screaming while whirling his shirt around. In mid-celebration he was suddenly confronted by a fan who had got on to the pitch. The supporter headed in for a cuddle but slipped over at the vital moment and Mitrovic did brilliantly to avoid an unfortunate collision, jumping high into the air and over him. Undaunted, the fan, who later got a banning order from Newcastle for his troubles, scrambled to his feet and claimed the hug, which bare-chested Mitrovic willingly shared.

Taking your shirt off when it's sure to cost you a booking has always seemed a pretty stupid thing to do. But no way could Sergio Aguero be blamed for getting caught up in the moment after scoring a 94th-minute winner for Manchester City against Queens Park Rangers, surely one of the most memorable goals of the 21st century. It was 10 May 2012, and City needed to win to clinch the club's first league title in 44 years. Aguero, at the end of his debut season in Manchester, won it with a super goal when a neat little dummy in the area left him free to smash the ball past keeper Paddy Kenny at his near post. The crowd went wild, and so too did Aguero, racing away with shirt whirled around his head. When his team-mates managed to catch him and drag him to the ground to join in his celebration they found he was crying just a little bit.

Mind you, Frenchman Eric Hassli of the Vancouver Whitecaps thought he had found a way around the no-removing-a-shirt law and would avoid a yellow card. When he scored he took off his shirt and threw it into the crowd, revealing an identical Whitecaps shirt underneath. But he was still cautioned – and as he'd already been booked he was sent off as well.

Of course, players have been known to remove items of clothing in the excitement of the moment. And what could be more exciting than having just won the World Cup? Never far from controversy, though, Gennaro Gattuso had to be stopped by FIFA officials from running round in his underpants after taking his shorts off in celebration when Italy won the 2006 World Cup.

Actually, it's not the only time the excitable Gattuso has been seen out in his under-crackers. He also took off his shorts – as you do – to celebrate with AC Milan fans that same year and join them in a few choruses of rude songs about the manager of rivals Inter Milan. Wait a minute, isn't this the same combative midfielder who took on Joe Jordan, of all people, during a Champions League match? Yes, that was Gattuso, who picked up a four-match ban for tangling with the legendarily tough guy, who was coaching Spurs at the time. Apparently, the verbal fisticuffs were conducted in broad Scots, the Italian having played for Rangers early in his career when he picked up a few useful expressions. Oh, and his wife's Scottish too.

Another player who took his shorts off to avoid a booking for removing his shirt was Mirko Vucinic, when he scored both goals for Juventus in a 2-1 win against Pescara in 2006. It didn't work – the referee booked him anyway, and his manager subbed him. Still, he wasn't deterred from his unusual celebration – Vucinic did it again after scoring for Montenegro in a Euro 2012 qualifying match against Switzerland, which his country won 1-0. That time, Vucinic celebrated in his white underpants, with his shorts perched on his head.

18

Opposition: When and when not to celebrate

CHOOSING NOT to celebrate when you've scored against your old club has become something of a tradition in football. Apart from Denis Law (Manchester City against his old club Manchester United), there was Frank Lampard scoring at the end of his playing career for Manchester City against his beloved Chelsea, Aaron Ramsey refusing to celebrate when scoring twice for Arsenal against his boyhood club Cardiff City, Cristiano Ronaldo after scoring for Real Madrid against Manchester United, Fernando Torres after scoring for Atletico Madrid against Liverpool, Jimmy Floyd Hasselbaink after scoring for Charlton at Chelsea, Cesc Fabregas after scoring for Chelsea against Arsenal, and Matt Le Tissier after one of his many goals for Southampton because his mate Tim Flowers was the opposition goalkeeper for Blackburn.

One of the saddest of non-celebrations was when Fabrizio Miccoli was in tears after scoring for Palermo in a 4-2 win over his home town club Lecce in the Italian league and had to be substituted at half-time. The story had a happy ending as the Italian international was later released by Palermo and went back to Lecce, where they made him captain.

One player who definitely didn't subscribe to the non-celebration rule was Emmanuel Adebayor in a highly controversial moment in Manchester City's 4-2 win against his old club Arsenal in 2009. Adebayor sprinted the length of the field after scoring to go down on his knees and celebrate in front of the Arsenal fans. Supporters often hate a former player more than any other and Adebayor's provocative actions were roundly condemned as having the potential to start a riot.

And to be fair, the man himself eloquently apologised after the game, offering the two-second rule in mitigation. He explained that two seconds is how long your emotions are out of control after scoring a goal. Not that Usain Bolt himself could have got from one end of the City of Manchester Stadium pitch to the other within the out-of-control period before common sense returned. Once all the hot air subsided and the passions died down, the Togo-born striker, who wears a wristband in the colours of the Togo flag and kisses it after scoring a goal, was given a suspended two-match ban for his actions.

By the time he arrived at his next club, Spurs, Adebayor's celebrations had matured into a dainty synchronised samba with Gareth Bale that could one day earn a spot on *Strictly Come Dancing*. Or possibly not. On another occasion at Spurs, Adebayor showed his gratitude to interim manager Tim Sherwood for recalling him to the side by scoring in the team's 5-1 win over Sunderland in April 2014. And he further showed it by going across to the bench and saluting the boss. And how did Sherwood respond? By saluting him back in return.

Sam Clucas 'did an Adebayor' when he scored for Stoke City against his old club Swansea on 25 January 2020. He'd been taunted all game by his former fans – 'what a waste of money' was one of the kinder things they were saying about him. So, when he scored the first in a 2-0 Stoke win, Clucas ignored his own fans and sprinted down to the other end where the away supporters were gathered. He was chased all the way by his team-mates but got there first, pointing to the name on his back in case any Swansea fans wondered who he was. Stoke manager Michael O'Neill helpfully pointed out afterwards: 'I think he was possibly getting a bit of stick for his time at Swansea, having been an ex-player.'

Whether to celebrate against your former club all depends on how you left them. That was what David Seaman told talkSPORT, having celebrated enthusiastically when his new club Manchester City scored against his old club Arsenal in 2003. He'd played more than 400 games for Arsenal, and was only at City for a season, but said the offer he received from Arsenal 'wasn't brilliant' and he felt he still had something to prove at City. He said: 'I was running around, giving it loads, and I noticed Thierry Henry looking at me. I was like "sorry, sorry, I got carried away!"'

Even though it wasn't relevant any more, Spanish international Michu brought his favourite celebration to the Premier League when he joined Swansea. It was to hold his hand over his ear and it evolved when rival fans in Spain teased him when he was playing for Celta Vigo against Granada and missed a penalty. He got his revenge when the teams met again in 2012, scoring the only goal of the game, and couldn't resist reminding opposition fans of the previous occasion. He told WalesOnline: 'I still like to do the celebration because it reminds me of my journey here.'

How old do you have to be before you answer this: 'At your age you should know better.' 21 perhaps? 25? Surely not 30? Well, that was how old Gary Neville was when he celebrated a goal and faced accusations that at 30 he should be beyond that sort of behaviour. Mind you, he did make a bit of a meal of his celebration, racing 60 yards down the pitch to cavort in front of opposition fans.

The celebration followed a last-minute winning goal at Old Trafford for Manchester United against bitter rivals Liverpool on 21 January 2006. Neville sprinted towards the away fans, leapt in the air, punched the sky, kissed his badge, and generally acted as if he was altogether pretty pleased. As he said afterwards: 'What are you meant to do? Smile sweetly and jog back to the halfway line?'

Neville paid a price for his taunts, incurring a £5,000 fine from the FA and a warning about his future conduct. Never short of an opinion or three, Neville risked further punishment by the authorities for criticising their decision. And in so doing, he stood up for anyone who has ever got in trouble for over-the-top celebrations. 'I am extremely disappointed,' he said. 'It's a poor decision, not just for me but for all footballers. Being a robot, devoid of passion and spirit, is obviously the way forward for the modern-day footballer.' Neville had vigorously denied a charge of improper conduct, pointing out that he had not made any rude gestures and claimed that he had been subjected to obscene chants from the Liverpool fans. What told against Neville was that players had been asked on police advice at the start of that season to avoid provocative celebrations for safety reasons.

United manager Sir Alex Ferguson was, as ever, fiercely vocal in defence of his captain, particularly against the whispered accusation that at the age of 30 Neville should have been showing a bit more restraint. After all, Sir Alex himself was still as passionate as ever before eventually retiring from management at the age of 72.

Some of the criticisms of Neville's behaviour were levelled at him by Liverpool stalwart Jamie Carragher – ten years on and they were the best of mates as pundits together on Sky Sports. Carragher himself played more than 700 games for Liverpool and was the club's second-longest-serving player ever, but he said he always had so many preparations to make for a game that there was no time to think about how he was going to celebrate a goal. He made up for it in retirement, though, and not many Liverpool goals went by without him at least punching the air and having a little cheer, even if he was broadcasting at the time.

Neville, meanwhile, had no plans to grow older gracefully after that badge-kissing moment. At the grand old age of 41, he showed his commitment as England coach by racing 50 metres up the touchline to join his team celebrating a last-minute winner against Wales in Euro 2016.

There was little Leeds United could do but hold their hands up and say sorry when a member of their coaching staff was caught spying at the training ground of their next opponents Derby County in January 2019. Leeds won the subsequent match 2-0 and midfielder Mateusz Klich celebrated by pretending he was looking through a pair of binoculars. Move on, nothing to see here. There was retribution in spades for Derby when the teams met again in the Championship play-off semi-finals four months later. Derby went through 4-3 on aggregate over the two-legger and – surprise, surprise – more than a few of their players rounded off the evening with a binoculars celebration. Touche.

Unlucky for Jayson Molumby when he scored what he thought was his first goal in senior football and celebrated with an elaborate little dance in which his upper body and shoulders seemed to do all the work. It was one of the three goals Millwall scored in an away win at Nottingham Forest in March 2020 but his colleague Matt Smith claimed he'd got the final touch as part of a hat-trick. Smith told journalists afterwards: 'I said sorry to Jayson. His celebration was worthy of a goal but I just got a touch on it.' Molumby tweeted: 'Don't care taking it first professional goal great win.' The Republic of Ireland youngster also had an insightful comment to SLP Media on celebrating a last-minute goal with windmilling arms in front of Charlton fans earlier in the season: 'It's just the moment. It's football, isn't it? You give a bit back, don't you? If they'd scored a last minute winner then you can be sure they would be giving it to our fans big time.'

Cocaine-snorting imitations, and political slogans under his shirt, Robbie Fowler was never short of a controversy in a long and often illustrious career. First, the cocaine bit. It came on a sunny Saturday in April 1999, when Fowler scored a penalty for Liverpool against Everton, a derby which is always an intense, frantic, no-holds-barred grudge match. Instead of trotting politely back to the centre circle, the England striker went down on his knees and pretended to sniff the white line of the penalty area. His manager, Gerard Houllier, said he thought it might have been a Cameroonian grass-eating celebration. But the rest of us recognised that as the lamest excuse ever and picked up the whiff of a cocaine analogy.

In a very humble apology afterwards, Fowler said it was aimed at Everton fans who taunted him as a drug abuser whenever he was out and about in the city. Liverpool went on to win the match 3-2 but Fowler came off the pitch to find he was in hot water. And not just from the after-match showers. His actions were reported to the police and he was also fined by his club. Then the FA stepped up and Fowler received a six-match ban, though two of those were for a separate incident, wiggling his backside at a Chelsea player, Graeme Le Saux, in a so-called homophobic taunt. Fowler later apologised to Le Saux and said he was just a young man – he was 23 – when he stepped out of line. Or went on all fours to sniff it, to be exact.

No stranger to controversy, Joey Barton was fined £2,000 by the FA for exposing his bare bottom to Everton fans after Manchester City had scored an injury-time equaliser against them in September 2006. Barton had received plenty of abuse from Everton supporters throughout the match and Merseyside police decided the gesture warranted no further action when it was reported to them. A couple of months later, Barton was much less provocative when he ran to the corner with City striker Bernardo Corradi after a goal against Fulham and knelt down while Corradi 'knighted' him with the corner flag.

A striker whose celebration ended with him red-faced and red-carded was Uruguayan international Edinson Cavani. His trademark move, which he explained was a tribute to his love of hunting and to the friends who helped foster it, was to drop on one knee and use an imaginary rifle to fire at the crowd. Playing for Paris Saint-Germain in October 2014, he converted a penalty in a 3-1 win over Lens and took aim in his sniper pose as usual. But the referee hated it, and booked him. An annoyed Cavani remonstrated with the official and made a bad situation worse, getting sent off for dissent. His club president Nasser Al-Khelaifi criticised the decision, saying that punishments for outlandish celebrations were bad for French football, and that Cavani should never have been booked in the first place for his rifle celebration as he always did it.

Another player who got sent off for over-celebrating after picking up a second yellow was a striker never far from controversy, Diego Costa. YouTube footage shows Costa relished a spicy dressing room celebration in his time at Chelsea and when he joined Atletico Madrid his over-the-top antics carried on while making his debut in January 2018. The Spanish international striker scored in the La Liga match with Getafe and seven minutes later got another one. He ran to celebrate with the front row of the crowd, hurdling the advertising hoardings to get there, and was booked for 'unsporting behaviour'. But he'd previously been yellow-carded for elbowing an opponent, so off he went. Even though his team had to play out the last half-hour with ten men, Costa's second goal still turned out to be the winner.

One hat-trick hero who later regretted his gun-toting celebration was Clive Mendonca, who was outstanding for Charlton when they won what's reckoned to be the most dramatic ever play-off final. It was the First Division play-off in 1998 and Mendonca's goals gave his team a 4-4 draw with Sunderland as they fought back from going behind three times. He then added a penalty in the subsequent 7-6 shoot-out to help Charlton land promotion. His hat-trick was the first in a Wembley final since Geoff Hurst more than 30 years earlier. Mendonca celebrated by firing pretend guns, but as a boyhood Sunderland fan who was born and raised in the area, he wished he hadn't done it and later apologised for what he said was a spur of the moment reaction.

Never far from the odd controversial moment in his career (or life), Southend striker Nile Ranger pretended to use his boot as a gun after scoring in his side's 4-2 victory at Fleetwood Town on 23 September 2017. He seemed to mime 'shooting' the crowd with it but explained later on Twitter: 'To put things straight I wasn't shooting the crowd. I just have a lot of ammunition in the boots this season.' So that's all right, then.

If a player's been getting stick from opposition fans, shouldn't he be allowed to get his revenge and celebrate in front of them if he's scored against their team? Rangers striker Alfredo Morelos was yellow-carded for doing just that in his team's 2-0 win at

Motherwell in December 2019 but it was his second booking of the game and meant he was sent off. It has to be said he looked slightly disappointed at the decision. Morelos told the *Scottish Sun*: 'I did not do that celebration with the intention of offending the opposition fans. I celebrate every goal with joy.'

Minutes after coming off the bench at Newcastle on 3 November 2018, Ayoze Perez headed the winner against Watford and had a little go at the fans who had booed his arrival by sticking his fingers in his ears. It felt good, so Perez kept it as his celebration when he moved on to Leicester. And, of course, he couldn't resist doing it when he scored for his new team against his old one, though some Newcastle fans were angry that he'd ignored the non-celebration tradition when scoring against a former club. There was a twist in the tale when Leicester lost 2-1 at home on 11 January 2020 to a Southampton team they'd thumped 9-0 earlier in the season, when Perez had enjoyed scoring a hat-trick. Defender Jack Stephens was pictured, yes, you've guessed it, grinning as he put his fingers in his ears. Revenge can be so sweet at times like that.

Arsenal once suspended one of their own players for his goal celebration. Full-back Sammy Nelson dropped his shorts after scoring against Coventry on 3 April 1979, having earlier put the ball through his own goal. He said his spur-of-the-moment gesture was to fans in the crowd who had barracked him for his previous mistake. Arsenal weren't prepared to turn a blind eye to Nelson's cheekiness and suspended him for a fortnight and fined him two weeks' wages.

Matheus Pereira was another player who was big enough to apologise for his goal celebration after putting West Bromwich Albion 2-0 up late in their game at Queens Park Rangers in October 2019. He dragged his fingers across his neck in a cut-throat gesture, intending to indicate that it was game over. But he found out afterwards the QPR stadium is named after an academy player who died from a stab wound. Pereira apologised on West Brom's official website: 'It was never my intention to cause offence. I am here to enjoy English football and make friends.'

It was hardly rock and roll, more rock-paper-scissors, but there was plenty of meaning when Christian Benteke and Mamadou Sakho acted out a goal celebration after Crystal Palace scored against Liverpool in April 2017 on their way to a 2-1 win at Anfield. Sakho was actually a Liverpool player on loan to Palace at the time so wasn't playing in the match. His little hand game with goalscorer Benteke showed where his loyalties lay and didn't go unnoticed by the Liverpool fans.

And it was no wonder team-mates Marco Fabian and Alberto Medina, playing for Guadalajara in the Mexican league in 2011, were soon having to say sorry for their badly-received goal celebration. One of them pretended to take out a pistol and shoot his colleague in the head. Celebrations based on gangland executions would probably be pretty controversial the world over, and it was certainly no joking matter in Mexico. The club fined them 50,000 Mexican pesos (more than £2,000) but both men paid double the fine and with team-mates also chipping in, they donated an even bigger sum to a local orphanage.

Scott Brown doesn't do anything by halves, and he landed in hot water after celebrating Celtic's win over Rangers on 31 March 2019. The club's captain was accused by the Scottish Football Association of 'failing to act in the best interest of Scottish football' after he celebrated in front of the away fans. But the hot water wasn't so warm after all and Brown was cleared of the charge.

Sometimes it's fans' celebrations which cause controversy, rather than the players' actions. Peter Crouch has a view on one enthusiastic supporter he always used to see at Bolton. In his book *How to be a Footballer*, the former England striker comments: 'Bolton used to have a bloke at the Reebok Stadium who would run about at the front of the stand waving a giant flag whenever they scored. Fireworks would go off. It really used to wind me up. I wanted to go in two-footed and take him out.'

19

Memories: Famous five

IT MIGHT have been because of the goals, the celebrations, the win itself, or, just as likely, the promise for the future that the performance provided (though, as we know about football, it's the hope that kills you). All of us have matches that have been landmarks in our football-following lives. The sort of occasion when you can remember exactly where you were when you watched it happen. I've picked five of mine from a lifetime of watching matches. I bet all of us would come up with something different, though I do have the dubious honour of being able to go back quite a lot further than many.

Here's my five:

1953. The 'Matthews Cup Final', and a 4-3 win for Blackpool over Bolton.

1966. England win the World Cup. Obviously.

1981. Spurs beat Manchester City in the FA Cup Final after a replay. Especially unforgettable because of seeing what players from different countries like

Ossie Ardiles and Ricky Villa could bring to our football.

1990. Italia 90 was great all the way through and a huge boost for our national game after a terrible decade. What a night to remember when England unluckily went out on penalties in the semi-final.

1999. Manchester United dramatically winning the Champions League with two late, late goals.

And there were others that were so close to making my shortlist. The confrontational 1970 FA Cup Final replay between Chelsea and Leeds, teams with a mutual disregard for each other – a full-back in our football team boasted that his parents were the proud owners of the only colour television we knew of, and 12 of us in his sitting room didn't seem wrong at the time. The disappointment of the 1973 World Cup qualifying match between England and Poland, which ended 1-1 despite the mighty Brian Clough telling us the opposition goalkeeper was a clown. Euro 96 in England, which was another case of so near, so far. England winning 5-1 in Germany (though I'd played cricket that afternoon and was still on my way home when the first goal flew in). Liverpool fighting back from three-down to Milan to win the 2005 Champions League in a penalty shoot-out. Sergio Aguero winning the Premier League for Manchester City in 2012 with a thrilling late winning goal. I hasten to add I don't claim to have been at these matches – all of them were seen through the glorious medium of television.

The first one of my five, the 1953 Cup Final, I only saw because one of my older brothers was invited by a friend to watch it on television (having a TV was not a given at the time) and I somehow persuaded him to take me along. I think I spent the afternoon playing with a Dinky car on the brown lino floor. Pathe News coverage of that iconic match shows there was some terrible goalkeeping, along with pretty vigorous chain-smoking on the terraces. There was also the unusual pre-substitute sight of an injured player hobbling on the left wing so his team didn't have to continue with ten players. And Bolton's crocked John Bell even bravely headed a goal from that position to put his side 3-1 up. Blackpool, inspired by Stanley Matthews – the man they called the Wizard of the Dribble – fought back in the second half with Matthews turning defenders inside out as he took them on. They were all-square by injury time but then Matthews set up the winner for Bill Perry from close range, with a little pull-back from the right wing. And the celebration? Pretty impressive and excited for the 1950s, all the outfield players bundling in with a lot of jumping and arm waving.

My first big game, and this I did see live in all its colourful, noisy, atmospheric, onion and peanut-smelling glory, was Millwall against Newcastle in the fourth round of the 1956/57 FA Cup. Many far-braver-than-me fans climbed the floodlight pylons for a lofty if dangerous view and there were 45,646 of us crammed into the rickety old Den that day. Millwall were just a Division Three South team, while mighty Newcastle were FA Cup giants, but the gap between them was bridged by Stan Anslow. Normally a full-back, he'd just been converted to a centre-forward and smashed in two goals for a memorable 2-1 win. And his celebration? Pretty animated with both hands up to the sky and a lovely running cuddle back towards the halfway line with the nearest team-mate.

My dad's habit was to get his sons to a game early so we'd get a good view (though Millwall fans would always pass youngsters over their heads, like crowd-surfing at a gig, so we could line up behind the pitch-side wall). We'd then have to leave ten minutes from the end to get at the front of the queue for the bus home. I always told myself that when I grew up the first thing I was going to do was learn to drive so I wouldn't have to leave matches early. My mum would have had a fit if she'd known what going to a match at Millwall was really like. Hard-swearing, rough, tough supporters who created a marvellously intimidating atmosphere for the opposition to endure. How great it felt to be one of them, though. Players like Harry Cripps were heroes because they'd run through brick walls for the club, but Charlie Hurley and, later, Keith Weller were also appreciated for the skills they brought to life with the Lions. There's some brief but beautiful grainy black-and-white footage from that memorable FA Cup tie, my first 'big match'. Happy days indeed.

Apart from realising just how good it felt to be a loyal part of the Millwall following – 'no one likes us, we don't care' – I found at this time just how much I anticipated the newspaper reports of the games I'd seen. All the games that had been played, really, but especially if I'd been there and wanted to see if my conclusions were the same as the professional reporter. I did a paper round for years and would read match reports in every available morning newspaper before shoving them through letter-boxes – one man even complained to my newsagent that his paper had been read before he received it. The joint love of football and newspapers propelled me into a career in journalism that I enjoyed for every single day of a long working life. How lucky was that.

As I said at the start of the chapter, I remember exactly where I was when England won the World Cup at Wembley on 30 July 1966. I was watching it on TV before going out in a flag-waving, horn-tooting convoy of cars driven by those of us old enough to have a licence. But I did go to one of the group stage matches, when England beat Mexico 2-0 and Bobby Charlton scored a terrific solo goal from fully 25 yards out. I liked his celebration, too, a big leap with a huge punch of the air while he was up there, both arms then raised high with a big smile on his face, before a nice embrace with the nearest team-mate, Terry Paine.

Considering what was at stake, the pinnacle of any footballer's career, the celebrations in the World Cup Final itself were pretty restrained. Both Geoff Hurst and Martin Peters jumped into the air after scoring against West Germany during the 90 minutes, which ended 2-2. But as was traditional in football at the time, the attitude was 'there's a nice goal, jolly good, but let's get on with the game again'. When Hurst got the clinching third goal in extra time, there was all that kerfuffle over whether it had crossed the line, so celebrations were put on hold while the imposing-looking linesman was consulted. It was like a VAR moment. And when he completed his hat-trick right at the end, a by now understandably knackered Hurst didn't do much more than lean into a congratulatory hug from Alan Ball. We knew it was all over by then.

Jump forward 15 years, but still at Wembley as Spurs beat Manchester City in a replayed FA Cup Final. No one at the time probably recognised the significance of a marvellous, memorable winning goal by Ricky Villa. He and Ossie Ardiles were lured to England after playing for Argentina in their 1978 World Cup victory, and were pioneers of bringing international class, charisma and innovation to our game. Where they came, players like Ronaldo, Henry, Cantona, Bergkamp and De Bruyne followed. To name but a few.

Villa had been substituted in the final the previous Saturday when Spurs and City met for the first time, but how he rewarded manager Keith Burkinshaw for keeping the faith by scoring twice in a 3-2 replay victory. The winner was a great goal, a mazy dribble into the area, eluding several tackles, before beating keeper Joe Corrigan from close range. Villa fell to the ground under the keeper's challenge as the ball went in, but that couldn't spoil the moment for him. He got up and sprinted off in celebration, getting almost to the halfway line before team-mates caught up with him. A top moment, and a significant one for the future of English football.

So, too, was Italia 90 a significant time for the game here. We all learned to love football again, whether it was the emotional Gazza's tears, Gary Lineker's telling look, or Bobby Robson's jig. The England team raised our spirits and our enthusiasm and so nearly went all the way to winning the 1990 World Cup. My favourite moment was David Platt's last-minute winning goal in extra time against Belgium in round two. Paul Gascoigne won a free kick in midfield and took it himself, dropping it into the penalty area where Platt cleverly spun round to follow its flight and volleyed it into the far corner. His celebration was modest, running to the goal line with both arms raised before sinking to his knees, where jubilant team-mates mobbed him. OK, so missed penalties meant we lost out in the end and were beaten by West Germany in the semi-finals, but the whole run to that stage was glorious. Better to have loved and lost than never to have loved at all.

That Platt's goal came after 119 hard-fought but goalless minutes made it so much more fun. Manchester United's win over Bayern Munich in the UEFA Champions League Final in Barcelona on 26 May 1999 matched it and then went one better.

Bayern led an end-to-end game 1-0 going into injury time but 36 seconds after the 90 minutes was up, substitute Teddy Sheringham struck a dramatic equaliser low into the bottom corner. Extra time beckoned but United weren't finished. Sheringham headed the ball down when United forced another corner and Ole Gunnar Solskjaer, the other sub, deflected it high into the net. It was, to be exact, 2 minutes 17 seconds into the added time and one of the most dramatic climaxes ever. Solskjaer slid away (as we saw earlier) in jubilation while at the other end, goalkeeper Peter Schmeichel performed a solo celebration with a perfectly executed cartwheel.

TV viewers voted this fourth in the Channel 4 programme *100 Greatest Sporting Moments* (well, since you ask, beaten only by Steve Redgrave's fifth Olympic gold medal, England winning the World Cup, and Germany 1 England 5). One hundred great moments – how lucky have any of us been to enjoy such a sporting life ...

20

Goalkeepers: Glass fronted

TO BE fair, it's not the greatest goal celebration, or by any means the longest. But it's got to be one of the most jubilant, with one of the largest number of people ever involved. All Jimmy Glass did after scoring the winner for Carlisle against Plymouth on 8 May 1999 was raise his right arm aloft and turn away in triumph. Within a fraction of a second he was mobbed and dragged to the ground by his team-mates, followed very shortly by dozens of delirious fans piling in on top. And to be fair to them all in their moment of madness, it was a pretty special goal. After all, Glass is a goalkeeper and was only on loan to Carlisle at the time because of an emergency. Previous goalkeeper Tony Caig had been sold to Blackpool and Richard Knight's loan period had been cut short due to injury.

It was the last minute of the last game of the season and Carlisle needed to win to stay in the Football League. Injury time had arrived with the score 1-1 when Carlisle forced a corner. Glass, who reckoned he scored a hat-trick in training the previous day, raced the length of the field to join in ... and the rest is history. The Plymouth goalkeeper parried Scott Dobie's goal-bound header but only to the red-shirted Glass, who advanced to smash it in on the half-volley from five yards out. Glass had been urged to go forward by his manager Nigel Pearson and his goal meant Carlisle got the win they needed and Scarborough were relegated to the Football Conference instead, after a 1-1 draw with Peterborough.

Cue mad celebrations, but Glass, having completed his third game on loan for Carlisle, never played for them again. It wasn't long after that he drifted out of full-time football, though his feat was remembered in 2014 when the Puma boots he was wearing that day were donated to the National Football Museum. And it's remembered by TV commentators who for years afterwards said, when a goalkeeper raced upfield for a last-minute corner: 'He's doing a Jimmy Glass!'

The closest Glass ever come to winning a medal in senior football was reaching the final of the Football League Trophy with Bournemouth at Wembley in 1998. But he scored an own goal and his team lost 2-1 to Grimsby. His Carlisle goal was ranked 72nd in that recently-mentioned greatest sporting moments TV programme. There are not many higher accolades than that – well just the 71, anyway.

Just a couple of weeks after the famous day in Carlisle, there was the extraordinary climax to the Champions League Final discussed in the previous chapter. And guess who did a Jimmy Glass and went up for the corner from which Manchester United equalised? Goalkeeper Peter Schmeichel. But he was told to stay back by manager Sir Alex Ferguson when United then won another corner from which they scored the winner. Cartwheels all round.

Normally, goalkeepers stay out of the way when their colleagues score, offering perhaps the occasional clenched fist salute and smug grin to the fans behind the goal. After all, it's a long way up to the other end to be the final one to join the celebratory pile-up. And a long way back, of course.

However, no one had apparently told keeper Pepe Reina what was the normal behaviour when Liverpool substitute David Ngog scored an injury-time goal against Manchester United on 25 October 2009. Reina raced from his area and astonishingly sprinted past all his other team-mates to become the first to congratulate the celebrating Ngog at the far end of the pitch.

And that wasn't the last time a Liverpool goalkeeper celebrated an injury-time goal to clinch a 2-0 win over deadly rivals Manchester United at Anfield. Spookily, the circumstances were identical when Alisson took off in unbridled delight as Liverpool advanced another step towards the 2019/20 Premier League title on 19 January 2020. They were leading by Virgil van Dijk's first-half headed goal when Alisson spotted Mo Salah lurking near the halfway line and United's defence undermanned by having too many players upfield looking for an equaliser. Alisson hit a pinpoint clearance and Salah did the rest, racing from halfway to steer the ball home. For a fraction of a second it looked as if a fan dressed top to tail in black had got on to the pitch. But it was just an excited Alisson, sprinting past high-fiving colleagues before knee-sliding up to Salah, the first Liverpool player to get there despite having had the furthest to run.

Nicky Weaver didn't appreciate what a significant moment it was for English football when he set off on a mad celebratory run behind the goal at Wembley. He'd just made the crucial save to give Manchester City a penalty shoot-out win over Gillingham in the 1999 Second Division promotion play-off. It took City from the depths of the third tier of English football back on their route to the top, that eventually saw them to four Premier League titles in seven years, starting in 2012. If they hadn't won that shoot-out, who knows how the next 20 years would have panned out?

The match itself, on 30 May 1999, was a thriller, Gillingham taking a two-goal lead after a goalless first 80 minutes. Some City fans stormed out at that moment, but their team hit back to level at 2-2 through Kevin Horlock and Paul Dickov. The equaliser from Dickov came in the final seconds of five minutes of added time and was scored against the best man at his wedding, Gillingham keeper Vince Bartram. Nice touch, that.

Into the shoot-out and Gillingham were trailing 3-1. If Guy Butters missed – or if 20-year-old Weaver saved – then City had won promotion. The keeper dived to his left to make the block, and set off on what he admitted later was a crazy run, leaping the advertising hoardings and racing across to where the City fans were also going mad, all the time beckoning his team-mates to join him. Weaver admitted many years later in an interview with the *Manchester Evening News*: 'I went on that silly run, didn't I? I've no idea what I was doing but I just didn't want it to end. I don't know where that stupid face came from, it was as though I was in a trance. It was brilliant, but it's caused me nothing but embarrassment since.'

As we've seen, some players have been known to shun a goal celebration, especially if it's against a team they used to play for, and Everton goalkeeper Tim Howard refused to celebrate on a windy night in January 2012 when he scored against Bolton. It wasn't that he'd ever played for them – he just felt sorry for the opposing goalkeeper. He scored his first professional goal with a massive wind-assisted clearance, making him only the fourth goalkeeper to score in a Premier League match since its formation in 1992. The American international described his goal as cruel and refused to celebrate out of sympathy for his beaten opposite number, Adam Bogdan.

He mentioned afterwards the 'goalkeepers' union' but as it turned out, Howard's goal and his non-celebration counted for nothing as Bolton hit back to win 2-1. They still went down at the end of that season, anyway.

Another goalkeeper who refused to celebrate out of respect for his opposite number one was Stoke City's Asmir Begovic. His 2013 goal against Southampton was meant to be just a clearance but at 97 yards it earned him a place in the Guinness World Records for the 'longest goal scored in football'. Longest and one of the quickest, too, as it came after just 13 seconds of the game, but Begovic declined to celebrate as he felt there-but-for-the-grace-of-God sympathy for Saints' beaten keeper Artur Boruc.

Running towards the bench, arms outstretched and grin even wider, Loris Angeli celebrated wildly when an opposition player hit the bar in a penalty shoot-out to decide the 2011 end-of-season promotion in one of the Italian lower leagues. He was the goalkeeper for Unione Sportiva Dro and when the penalty was missed it meant the shoot-out stayed at 4-4. But as he ran off to celebrate, poor old Loris didn't realise the ball had actually come down off the bar, bounced, spun back, and rolled oh so gently over the line. Obviously, his team-mate missed the next penalty and it was opponents Termeno who went up instead. Stay on your line next time, Loris – if there is a next time – and wait for the fat lady to sing.

It was down in non-league that I saw a memorable non-celebration by a goalscoring goalkeeper. Steve Williams went upfield for a last-minute corner when his team, Sittingbourne, were losing 3-2 away to Metropolitan Police in October 2006. The ball reached Williams lurking at the far post and he headed in the equaliser. Modest as they come, the keeper decided just to turn and sprint back to his own goal. But he's a big lad and he didn't make it much more than 20 yards before every one of his team-mates overhauled him and bundled him to the ground. His bravado in thinking he could outrun ten probably fitter and younger colleagues had to be admired, though.

There's an old saying that you don't have to be mad to be a goalkeeper, but it helps. Robert Kidiaba was an international keeper and his trademark goal celebration was really weird. Mad even. It was a so-called bum shuffle, bouncing around his area on his bottom, keeping the momentum going by digging in his heels and pushing out his hands.

The Democratic Republic of Congo international is now an MP in his own country and a charity worker.

How sweet, but when Bayern Munich's Dante scored against Freiburg in February 2014, he ignored all his team-mates and ran the length of the field to jump into the arms of goalkeeper Manuel Neuer. Because goalkeepers don't normally get to celebrate goals, he reckoned.

Saulo, a Brazilian goalkeeper, should have learned from the examples of fellow keepers in how to keep it down when they've scored. He went upfield and scored an injury-time winner for his team in 2011, only to get mobbed by his mates and tear ligaments in his knee, putting him out of the game for six months. He ruefully reflected: 'Yesterday I was so happy, today I'm so sad. But I'll recover.'

Getting promoted to Italy's Serie A in 2011 after his club had been out of it for 55 years is worth a moment or two of letting your hair down. Novara's Alberto 'Jimmy' Fontana thought so anyway, knocking down a backdrop set up for TV, kissing a reporter who was conducting an interview, and then running around without his shorts while letting off a fire extinguisher. Quite a celebration. And the goalkeeper was only an unused sub that day.

21

A job well done

WHAT'S THE most popular celebration of a goal in the Premier League? Well, thanks to Bill Edgar of *The Times* at least we know what they were for the first couple of months of 2019, as he kept a record of what happened when the first 245 goals were scored.

And the answer was: both arms out wide. In that period, 50 goals were celebrated that way, and, fair enough, as it's the most natural thing to do. Nothing planned, nothing fussy, just sheer joy at a job well done. Runners-up were: 49 leap into the air with arms thrown up; 27 knee slide; 12 point to assister (Manchester City's favourite); 12 carry the ball back to your own half (de rigueur if your team's losing). Beyond them, according to Bill's research, were: wag finger, beat chest, point to sky (especially if someone close to the player had recently died), dance, blow a kiss to the crowd, salute the crowd, kick or punch the corner flag, make a heart shape, acrobatics, point to a team-mate to get the ball out of the net, jump over the perimeter advertising board, cup an ear, put finger on lips to 'Ssh', suck a thumb, take off shirt.

So we've covered celebrations that are pre-planned, accidental, pointed, sexy, funny, political and even dangerous. And many more. But, in truth, most modern-day goals end with the scorer leading a charge towards their team's most vocal fans and happily celebrating in front of them. Probably preceded by a knee slide, always accompanied by lots of shouting, and sometimes everyone piling on top of each other. It's no coincidence that the players head for the supporters, as it's their chance to get as close to them as they're ever likely to. To say, 'thanks for being here, thanks for loving our club, thanks for spending your hard-earned money to follow us. Here's us showing our gratitude to you.' For leading 21st-century footballers are segregated from their fans by high security on their training grounds and even bigger fences around their mansions. They might do the school run but they're not often spotted in their local supermarket pushing a trolley for the weekly shop.

It wasn't always this way. As a boy, I was on the number 75 bus going to watch Charlton when their star forward, Johnny Summers, got on and sat next to me. The very same Johnny Summers who in 1957 scored five goals in an extraordinary 7-6 win over Huddersfield as Charlton fought back from 5-1 down with half an hour to go and ten men on the field. Everyone on the top deck of the bus that day knew it was Summers and that he was on his way to play in the game they were on their way to watch. Shy little me just stared out of the window and never even acknowledged my new best friend next to me. Tragically, Summers died of cancer a few years later at the age of 34.

Spurs players in the 1960s were encouraged by manager Bill Nicholson to spend some time in the pub after a game, mixing with the fans and discussing what had gone on. Don't suppose they needed a second invitation to do that. Footballers back then would often go on to run pubs after retiring, and there was definitely a drinking culture associated with the game. Bonding, they might have liked to call it, and it reached a peak in the 1980s and 1990s. It was frowned upon to go out the night before a game, but for the rest of the week a few pints a night – or down the pub after training – was the norm for many top players.

Managers like Arsene Wenger turned the tide. Players who had come through club youth systems were better disciplined, while more and more foreign players arrived with no background of exposure to drink. There was no more turning up for training with hangovers – players became more athletic, and fitness and nutritional experts came on board to make sure standards were accurately measured and then religiously kept. Even though Wenger was a pioneering new style of manager, all-conquering Arsenal had just a few years previously won the league and subsequently both major cup competitions. And that was even though at least two of that successful team had problems with drink. Captain Tony Adams was one of them and his battle with alcoholism was graphically detailed in his book *Addicted*. Yet he was still a terrific footballer and he was the hero when Arsenal beat deadly rivals Spurs in the 1993 FA Cup semi-final at Wembley, scoring the only goal of the game in the 79th minute.

The assist to the goal came from Paul Merson, and he captured the moment in celebration as he mimed what he was going to do afterwards. He used both hands to pretend to be drinking pint after pint of lager, all the time with his thirst-imitating tongue out and a big knowing grin on his face. Within a year Merson was publicly conceding addictions to alcohol, gambling and cocaine. After a suitable break, he successfully resumed his playing career and when that ended he extended his life in football by becoming a Sky Sports pundit where, among other things, he spoke eloquently about mental health issues in sport.

It was a similar story for the greatest goalscorer in English football. That's an official statistic, by the way, as Jimmy Greaves holds the record as the highest goalscorer in the history of English top-flight football. He, too, declared himself a recovering alcoholic more than 40 years ago but he went on to enjoy a terrific second career working on TV and in newspapers as an amusing and insightful football expert. And he once said he was prouder of his work in the media than of his playing career, as football had come easy to him.

Incidentally, hundreds of Greaves' goal celebrations matched his personality in being restrained and modest, though he did treat himself occasionally to a warm rubbing together of his hands.

Going back to Paul Merson, he had more in common with Paul Gascoigne than just their first names. They played in the same era and both could be filed under the category 'flawed genius'. And both performed on-field celebrations linked to alcohol which in retrospect might look inappropriate, though at least they showed an ability to laugh at themselves. It wouldn't have been called LOL back in 1996 when Gascoigne performed the famous celebration described in the opening chapter. But it was funny at the time and remains so to this day. It was also clever, topical, succinct and memorable.

And, of course, it followed a brilliant goal. Scored at a crucial time in a vital game against a traditional footballing enemy. The celebration was a response to the over-the-top holier-than-thou newspaper criticism levelled at the players. And from spoiled, overpaid brats they suddenly transformed into warm-hearted, joyous human beings. Of course, the golden moment had been cleverly pre-planned – as is frequently the way with the very best celebrations. Why were water bottles oh so handily lying around behind the goal? How come the players knew exactly what to do?

It was wonderful that Gascoigne scored such an exquisite goal as he was just the man to carry it off. He always played with his heart on his sleeve and was loved by one and all. Mind you, there was a time when he wasn't quite so revered and popular, and one ill-judged action ended with him receiving IRA death threats. While at Glasgow Rangers in the late 1990s, he pretended to play a flute during a game against arch rivals Celtic. The flute is a Loyalist symbol and the action was extremely provocative to the traditionally Catholic supporters of Celtic. Rangers manager Walter Smith said Gascoigne was disciplined for his actions, adding: 'There are always bits and pieces of him that let him down now and again.' The death threats were taken so seriously that police gave Gascoigne, who later apologised for his actions, a special mirrored device to check under his car for bombs.

While Gazza wound up the opposition fans, the boot was on the other foot a few years later when Celtic goalkeeper Artur Boruc took it upon himself to become a hate figure for Rangers supporters. He got in trouble for making gestures at them and another time for waving a Celtic flag, and in 2008 was even the subject of a complaint by an MP in the House of Commons for celebrating a Celtic win by wearing a t-shirt with God Bless the Pope on it.

Gascoigne wouldn't have been the man – or player – he was without the controversies and provocations. But for all that, his 1996 Wembley goal celebration was a special moment. A Number One in football.

Bibliography

Adams T., Ridley I., *Addicted* (HarperCollins, 1998).

Beckham, D. and Watt, T., *David Beckham: My Side – The Autobiography* (Hachette UK, 2013)

Bullard, J., *Bend It Like Bullard* (Hachette UK, 2014).

Crouch, P., *How to be a Footballer* (Random House, 2018).

Ferdinand R. with Custis S., *Rio: My Story* (Headline, 2006).

Goss J. and Couzens-Lake E., *Gossy The Autobiography* (Amberley Publishing, 2014).

Hewitt, P. and McGuigan P., *The Greatest Footballer You Never Saw: The Robin Friday Story* (Random House, 2011)

Hornby, N., *Fever Pitch* (Gallancz, 1992).

Index

INDEX